WOOL STUDIO

THE knit.wear CAPSULE COLLECTION

Interweave

fw

www.fwcommunity.com

22 21 20 19 18   5 4 3 2 1

SRN: 18KN03
ISBN-13: 978-1-63250-641-2

EDITORIAL DIRECTOR: KERRY BOGERT
EDITOR: MAYA ELSON
ART DIRECTOR: ASHLEE WADESON
COVER AND INTERIOR DESIGNER: KARLA BAKER
PHOTOGRAPHER: HARPER POINT PHOTOGRAPHY

CONTENTS

INTRODUCTION

Welcome to the first *Wool Studio* print compilation, assembled for people who love beautiful books and modern knitwear. For those of you new to *Wool Studio*, this is a capsule-collection series for the modern woman featuring sophisticated, simple, and luxurious knitwear. We've paired talented designers with exceptional yarns to bring you a chic and timeless collection of knits. *Wool Studio* was Interweave's first all-digital look-book series—the premier of Volume I received an enthusiastic reception, but we also heard the feedback from all our "book people" who wanted a print copy of their favorite new designs. So here it is, the first two volumes of *Wool Studio*, bound in hardcover and printed for your coffee table and knitting library.

The concept for *Wool Studio* is simple: less is more. We wanted simple silhouettes and intuitive designs that would let the fibers shine on a stripped-down canvas. In the *Wool Studio* series, every design element has purpose: to enhance and showcase the yarn. The gorgeous yarns are courtesy of Woolfolk, Shibui Knits, Sugar Bush, Kelbourne Woolens, Kingfisher Yarn & Fibre, Skacel, Universal Yarn, Fairmount Fibers, Mango Moon, Malabrigo, June Cashmere, Imperial Yarn, Plymouth Yarn, Trendsetter Yarns, Ancient Arts Fibre Crafts, Mrs. Crosby, Bare Naked Wools, and Valley Yarns—many thanks to them for making this collection possible.

The knitwear design in this collection is nothing short of stellar. We have been overwhelmed by the skill, thoughtfulness, and care that each designer poured into her work. It has been a thrill to work on these collections with Bristol Ivy, Emma Welford, Mary Anne Benedetto, Linda Marveng, Amy Gunderson, Sarah Solomon, Véronik Avery, Norah Gaughan, Kate Gagnon Osborn, Lana Jois, Amanda Bell, Andrea Babb, Susanna IC, Kephren Pritchett, Grace Akhrem, and Amanda Scheuzger. *Wool Studio* would not be what it is without each of their contributions.

But above all, this collection was created for you, dear knitter. Much like its mother title, *knit.wear*, *Wool Studio* is a slow fashion retreat—a place for reflection, simplicity, and clarity. We selected each of these designs with minimalism in mind, so that the process of making the projects—from selecting the yarn, to knitting, to wearing the finished piece for the season—is an experience that brings joy and serenity.

Wool Studio is for those who pause for slow fashion, conscientiously select their fibers, and seek contemporary designs made to outlast ephemeral trends. Look through these pages to find comfort, escape, and elegance worthy of the modern knitter.

MEGHAN BABIN
EDITOR, *INTERWEAVE KNITS* MAGAZINE

THE PATTERNS

CARMEL-
BY-THE-SEA

PULLOVER

Lana Jois

Textured, oversized, comfortable, and visually appealing—the Carmel-by-the-Sea Pullover is a versatile wardrobe staple that can be paired with herringbone trousers and leggings alike. The body of this pullover is worked in the round to the underarm, then the front and back are worked separately back and forth.

FINISHED SIZE

38½ (41½, 46, 50, 54½, 58¼)" (98 [105.5, 117, 127, 138.5, 148] cm) bust circumference. Pullover shown measures 41½" (105.5 cm); modeled with 7½" (19 cm) of positive ease.

YARN

Worsted weight (#4)

SHOWN HERE: Sugar Bush Yarns Bold (100% extrafine superwash merino; 190 yd [174 m]/ 3½ oz [100 g]): #3024 pulp mill, 6 (6, 7, 8, 8, 9) balls.

NEEDLES

Size U.S. 7 (4.5 mm): 16" and 32" circular (cir) and set of double-pointed (dpn).

Size U.S. 8 (5 mm): 32" cir and set of dpn.

Adjust needle size if necessary to obtain the correct gauge.

NOTIONS

Markers (m); stitch holders; tapestry needle.

GAUGE

17 sts and 24 rnds = 4" (10 cm) in Broken Rib on larger needle.

NOTES

- The body of this pullover is worked in the round to the underarm, then the front and back are worked separately back and forth.

- The sleeves are worked in the round from the bottom up.

STITCH GUIDE

**BROKEN RIB IN ROUNDS
(EVEN NUMBER OF STS)**

RND 1: *K1, p1; rep from * to end.

RND 2: Knit.

Rep Rnds 1 and 2 for patt.

**BROKEN RIB IN ROWS
(ODD NUMBER OF STS)**

ROW 1: (RS) *K1, p1; rep from * to last st, k1.

ROW 2: (WS) Purl.

Rep Rows 1 and 2 for patt.

INSTRUCTIONS

BODY

With smaller, longer cir needle, CO 164 (176, 196, 212, 232, 248) sts. Place marker (pm) and join in the rnd.

Work in k1, p1 rib for 1½" (3.8 cm). Change to larger needle. Work Broken Rib in rnds (see Stitch Guide) until piece measures 14 (14, 14½, 15¼, 15¾, 15¼)" (35.5 [35.5, 37, 38.5, 40, 38.5] cm) from CO, ending with Rnd 2 of patt, and ending 3 (3, 3, 5, 5, 5) sts before end of rnd on last rnd.

DIVIDE FOR FRONT AND BACK

NEXT RND: BO 5 (5, 5, 9, 9, 9) sts, work Row 1 of Broken Rib in rows (see Stitch Guide) over 77 (83, 93, 97, 107, 115) sts (including st rem on right needle after BO) and place these sts on holder for back, BO 5 (5, 5, 9, 9, 9) sts, work Row 1 of Broken Rib in rows to end—77 (83, 93, 97, 107, 115) sts rem for front.

FRONT

Work even in patt until armhole measures 3 (2¾, 2¾, 3, 3½, 3½)" (7.5 [7, 7, 7.5, 9, 9] cm), ending with a RS row.

SHAPE NECK

NOTE: *Shoulder shaping beg before neck shaping ends; read the foll section all the way through before proceeding.*

NEXT ROW: (WS) P35 (39, 44, 45, 50, 55), pm, p7 (5, 5, 7, 7, 5), pm, purl to end.

SHAPING ROW: (RS) Work in patt to 3 sts before m, k2tog, k1, sl m, M1R, work in patt to m, M1L, sl m, k1, ssk, work in patt to end—2 sts inc'd between m and 1 st dec'd at each side; no change to st count.

Rep shaping row every RS row 14 (16, 16, 16, 16, 18) more times, working new sts into patt between m and keeping first 2 sts outside m in St st—37 (39, 39, 41, 41, 43) sts between m.

At the same time, when armhole measures 7 (7½, 7½, 7¾, 8¼, 8¾)" (18 [19, 19, 19.5, 21, 22] cm), ending with a WS row, shape shoulders as foll: BO 6 (7, 9, 9, 11, 12) sts at beg of next 4 (4, 6, 4, 6, 6) rows, then BO 8 (8, 0, 10, 0, 0) sts at beg of foll 2 (2, 0, 2, 0, 0) rows—37 (39, 39, 41, 41, 43) sts rem.

Place sts on holder.

BACK

Return 77 (83, 93, 97, 107, 115) held sts to needle and, with WS facing, rejoin yarn.

Work in patt until armhole measures 7 (7½, 7½, 7¾, 8¼, 8¾)" (18 [19, 19, 19.5, 21, 22] cm), ending with a WS row.

SHAPE SHOULDERS

BO 6 (7, 9, 9, 11, 12) sts at beg of next 4 (4, 6, 4, 6, 6) rows, then BO 8 (8, 0, 10, 0, 0) sts at beg of foll 2 (2, 0, 2, 0, 0) rows—37 (39, 39, 41, 41, 43) sts rem. Place sts on holder.

SLEEVES

With smaller dpn, CO 38 (38, 38, 44, 44, 44) sts. Pm and join in the rnd.

Work in k1, p1 rib for 2" (5 cm).

Change to larger dpn. Work Broken Rib in Rounds for 2 rnds.

INC RND: K1, M1L, work in patt to end, M1R—2 sts inc'd.

Rep inc rnd every 10 (8, 8, 8, 8, 6)th rnd 8 (10, 9, 8, 2, 6) more times, then every 8 (6, 6, 6, 6, 4)th rnd 2 (2, 3, 2, 10, 8) times, working new sts into patt—60 (64, 64, 66, 70, 74) sts.

Work even until piece measures 20 (19½, 19, 18½, 18, 17½)" (51 [49.5, 48.5, 47, 45.5, 44.5] cm) from CO, ending with Rnd 1 of patt. BO all sts.

FINISHING

Weave in ends. Block pieces to measurements. Sew shoulder seams. Sew sleeves into armholes.

NECKBAND

Place front and back neck sts onto smaller 16" cir needle, with beg of rnd 1 st before left shoulder seam—74 (78, 78, 82, 82, 86) sts. Pm and join in the rnd.

NEXT RND: K2tog or p2tog as needed to maintain patt (last st of back neck and first st of front neck), work 35 (37, 37, 39, 39, 41) sts in patt, k2tog or p2tog as needed to maintain patt (last st of front neck and first st of back neck), work in patt to end—72 (76, 76, 80, 80, 84) sts rem.

Beg with Rnd 2, work Broken Rib in Rounds until neckband measures 2" (5 cm), ending with Rnd 1.

BO all sts.

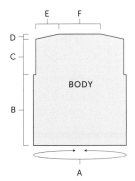

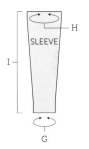

A: 38½ (41½, 46, 50, 54½, 58¼)" (98 [105.5, 117, 127, 138.5, 148] cm)

B: 14 (14, 14½, 15¼, 15¾, 15¼)" (35.5 [35.5, 37, 38.5, 40, 38.5] cm)

C: 7 (7½, 7½, 7¾, 8¼, 8¾)" (18 [19, 19, 19.5, 21, 22] cm)

D: 1" (2.5 cm)

E: 4¾ (5¼, 6¼, 6½, 7¾, 8½)" (12 [13.5, 16, 16.5, 19.5, 21.5] cm)

F: 8¾ (9¼, 9¼, 9¾, 9¾, 10)" (22 [23.5, 23.5, 25, 25, 25.5] cm)

G: 9 (9, 9, 10¼, 10¼, 10¼)" (23 [23, 23, 26, 26, 26] cm)

H: 14 (15, 15, 15½, 16½, 17½)" (35.5 [38, 38, 39.5, 42, 44.5] cm)

I: 20 (19½, 19, 18½, 18, 17½)" (51 [49.5, 48.5, 47, 45.5, 44.5] cm)

FALMOUTH

CARDIGAN

Kate Gagnon Osborn

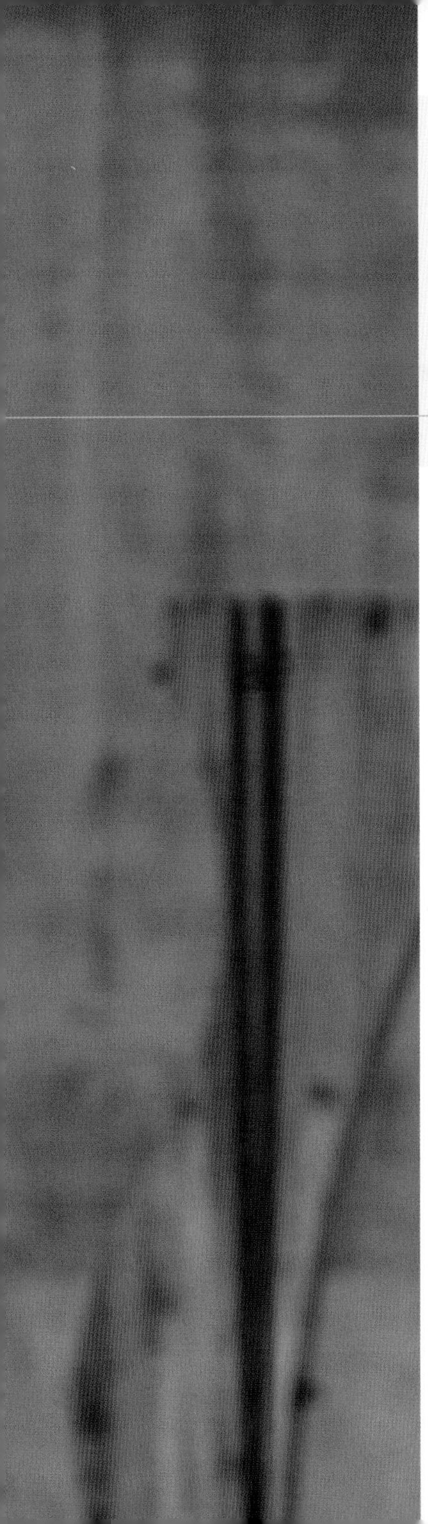

With its simple dolman-sleeve construction and generously proportioned collar, the Falmouth Cardigan is the perfect showcase for this wool-cashmere-silk blend yarn. The simple stockinette-stitch canvas makes the rich tweed pop, and the plump stitches let you finish this project quickly for instant gratification.

FINISHED SIZE

40 (44½, 49, 51½, 56, 60½)" (101.5 [113, 124.5, 131, 156] cm) hip measurement. Cardigan shown measures 44½" (113 cm); modeled with 8½" (21.5 cm) of positive ease.

YARN

Worsted weight (#4)

SHOWN HERE: The Fibre Co. Arranmore (80% merino wool, 10% cashmere, 10% silk; 175 yd [160 m]/3½ oz [100 g]): glenveagh castle, 5 (5, 6, 6, 6, 7) skeins.

NEEDLES

Size U.S. 8 (5 mm): 60" circular (cir) and set of double-pointed (dpn).

Size U.S. 9 (5.5 mm): 40" cir.

Adjust needle size if necessary to obtain the correct gauge.

NOTIONS

Markers (m); stitch holders; tapestry needle.

GAUGE

14 sts and 20 rows = 4" (10 cm) in St st on larger needle.

NOTES

- This cardigan is worked in pieces from the bottom up and seamed.

STITCH GUIDE

BROKEN RIB PATTERN:
(MULTIPLE OF 4 STS + 2)

ROW 1: (RS) Knit.

ROW 2: (WS) P2, *k2, p2; rep from * to end.

Rep Rows 1 and 2 for patt.

INSTRUCTIONS

BACK

With smaller cir needle, CO 70 (78, 86, 90, 98, 106) sts. Do not join.

Work in Broken Rib patt (see Stitch Guide) for 5" (12.5 cm), ending with a WS row.

Change to larger needle. Shape center back curve using short-rows as foll, working wraps tog with wrapped sts when you come to them as foll:

SHORT-ROW 1: (RS) Knit to last 24 sts, wrap next st, turn.

SHORT-ROW 2: (WS) Purl to last 24 sts, wrap next st, turn.

SHORT-ROW 3: Knit to last 16 sts, wrap next st, turn.

SHORT-ROW 4: Purl to last 16 sts, wrap next st, turn.

SHORT-ROW 5: Knit to last 8 sts, wrap next st, turn.

SHORT-ROW 6: Purl to last 8 sts, wrap next st, turn.

SHORT-ROW 7: Knit to end.

Work even in St st over all sts until piece measures 9" (23 cm) from CO at side edges and 10½" (26.5 cm) from CO in center, ending with a WS row.

SHAPE DOLMAN SLEEVES

INC ROW: (RS) K2, M1R, knit to last 2 sts, M1L, k2—2 sts inc'd.

Working new sts in St st, rep inc row every RS row 10 more times—92 (100, 108, 112, 120, 128) sts.

Work 1 WS row even.

NEXT ROW: (RS) Using the backward-loop method, CO 7 sts, knit to end—99 (107, 115, 119, 127, 135) sts.

NEXT ROW: CO 7 sts, purl to end—106 (114, 122, 126, 134, 142) sts.

Work even until armhole measures 6" (15 cm) above last sleeve CO row and 19¾" (50 cm) from CO at each side, ending with a WS row.

Shape shoulders using short-rows as foll:

SHORT-ROW 1: (RS) Knit to last 2 sts, wrap next st, turn.

SHORT-ROW 2: (WS) Purl to last 2 sts, wrap next st, turn.

SHORT-ROW 3: Knit to 2 sts before wrapped st, wrap next st, turn.

SHORT-ROW 4: Purl to 2 sts before wrapped st, wrap next st, turn.

Rep last 2 short-rows 4 (2, 0, 0, 0, 0) more times.

SHORT-ROW 5: Knit to 3 sts before wrapped st, wrap next st, turn.

SHORT-ROW 6: Purl to 3 sts before wrapped st, wrap next st, turn.

Rep last 2 short-rows 4 (6, 7, 7, 8, 8) more times.

SHORT-ROW 7: Knit to 4 sts before wrapped st, wrap next st, turn.

SHORT-ROW 8: Purl to 4 sts before wrapped st, wrap next st, turn.

Rep last 2 short-rows 1 (1, 3, 3, 3, 3) more time(s).

SHORT-ROW 9: Knit to 5 sts before wrapped st, wrap next st, turn.

SHORT-ROW 10: Purl to 5 sts before wrapped st, wrap next st, turn.

Rep last 2 short-rows 0 (0, 0, 0, 0, 1) more time.

NEXT ROW: Knit to end, working wraps tog with wrapped sts.

NEXT ROW: Purl to end, working wraps tog with wrapped sts—armhole measures 6½" (16.5 cm) above last sleeve CO.

Place sts on holder. Break yarn, leaving a 75" (190.5 cm) tail.

LEFT FRONT

With smaller cir needle, CO 19 (23, 27, 31, 35, 39) sts. Do not join.

ROW 1: (RS) Knit.

ROW 2: (WS) P3, *k2, p2; rep from *.

Rep Rows 1 and 2 until piece measures 5" (12.5 cm) from CO, ending with a RS row.

Change to larger needle. Shape center front curve using short-rows as foll, working wraps tog with wrapped sts when you come to them:

SHORT-ROW 1: (WS) Purl to last 13 (14, 16, 17, 18, 20) sts, wrap next st, turn.

SHORT-ROW 2: (RS) Knit to end.

SHORT-ROW 3: Purl to last 6 (7, 9, 10, 11, 13) sts, wrap next st, turn.

SHORT-ROW 4: Knit to end.

NEXT ROW: (WS) Purl to end.

Work even until piece measures 9" (23 cm) from CO at side edge (beg of RS rows), ending with a WS row.

SHAPE DOLMAN SLEEVE

INC ROW: (RS) K2, M1R, knit to end—1 st inc'd.

Working new sts in St st, rep inc row every RS row 10 more times—30 (34, 38, 42, 46, 50) sts.

Work 1 WS row even.

NEXT ROW: (RS) Using the backward-loop method, CO 7 sts, knit to end—37 (41, 45, 49, 53, 57) sts.

Work even until armhole measures 6" (15 cm) above sleeve CO row, ending with a RS row.

Shape shoulder using short-rows as foll:

SHORT-ROW 1: (WS) Purl to last 2 sts, wrap next st, turn.

SHORT-ROW 2: (RS) Knit to end.

SHORT-ROW 3: Purl to 2 sts before wrapped st, wrap next st, turn.

SHORT-ROW 4: Knit to end.

Rep last 2 short-rows 4 (2, 0, 0, 0, 0) more times.

SHORT-ROW 5: Purl to 3 sts before wrapped st, wrap next st, turn.

SHORT-ROW 6: Knit to end.

Rep last 2 short-rows 4 (6, 7, 7, 8, 8) more times.

SHORT-ROW 7: Purl to 3 (4, 3, 4, 4, 4) sts before wrapped st, wrap next st, turn.

SHORT-ROW 8: Knit to end.

Rep last 2 short-rows 1 (1, 3, 3, 3, 3) more time(s).

SHORT-ROW 9: Purl to 4 (4, 4, 5, 5, 5) sts before wrapped st, wrap next st, turn.

SHORT-ROW 10: Knit to end.

Rep last 2 short-rows 0 (0, 0, 0, 0, 1) more time—depending on your size, last wrapped st is either the edge st or the st next to it.

NEXT ROW: (WS) Purl to end, working wraps tog with wrapped sts.

NEXT ROW: Knit—armhole measures 6½" (16.5 cm) above last sleeve CO.

Place sts on holder. Break yarn.

RIGHT FRONT

With smaller cir needle, CO 19 (23, 27, 31, 35, 39) sts. Do not join.

ROW 1: (RS) Knit.

ROW 2: (WS) *P2, k2; rep from * to last 3 sts, p3.

Rep Rows 1 and 2 until piece measures 5" (12.5 cm) from CO, ending with a WS row.

Change to larger needle. Shape center front curve using short-rows as foll, working wraps tog with wrapped sts when you come to them:

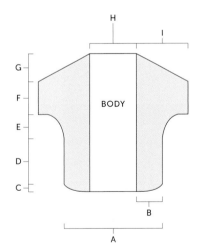

A: 20 (22¼, 24½, 25¾, 28, 30¼)" (51 [56.5, 62, 65.5, 71, 77] cm)

B: 5½ (6½, 7¾, 8¾, 10, 11¼)" (14 [16.5, 19.5, 22, 25.5, 28.5] cm)

C: 1½" (3.8 cm)

D: 9" (23 cm)

E: 4¾" (12 cm)

F: 6½" (16.5 cm)

G: 5½ (5½, 6, 6, 6½, 6¾)" (14 [14, 15, 15, 16.5, 17] cm)

H: 9¼ (9¼, 9¼, 8, 8, 8)" (23.5 [23.5, 23.5, 20.5, 20.5, 20.5] cm)

I: 10½ (11¾, 12¾, 14, 15¼, 16¼)" (26.5 [30, 32, 35.5, 38.5, 41.5] cm)

SHORT-ROW 1: (RS) Knit to last 13 (14, 16, 17, 18, 20) sts, wrap next st, turn.

SHORT-ROW 2: (WS) Purl to end.

SHORT-ROW 3: Knit to last 6 (7, 9, 10, 11, 13) sts, wrap next st, turn.

SHORT-ROW 4: Purl to end.

NEXT ROW: (RS) Knit to end.

Work even until piece measures 9" (23 cm) from CO at side edge (end of RS rows), ending with a WS row.

SHAPE DOLMAN SLEEVE

INC ROW: (RS) Knit to last 2 sts, M1L, k2—1 st inc'd. Working new sts in St st, rep inc row every RS row 10 more times—30 (34, 38, 42, 46, 50) sts.

NEXT ROW: (WS) Using the backward-loop method, CO 7 sts, purl to end—37 (41, 45, 49, 53, 57) sts.

Work even until armhole measures 6" (15 cm) above sleeve CO row, ending with a WS row.

Shape shoulder using short-rows as foll:

SHORT-ROW 1: (RS) Knit to last 2 sts, wrap next st, turn.

SHORT-ROW 2: (WS) Purl to end.

SHORT-ROW 3: Knit to 2 sts before wrapped st, wrap next st, turn.

SHORT-ROW 4: Purl to end.

Rep last 2 short-rows 4 (2, 0, 0, 0, 0) more times.

SHORT-ROW 5: Knit to 3 sts before wrapped st, wrap next st, turn.

SHORT-ROW 6: Purl to end.

Rep last 2 short-rows 4 (6, 7, 7, 8, 8) more times.

SHORT-ROW 7: Knit to 3 (4, 3, 4, 4, 4) sts before wrapped st, wrap next st, turn.

SHORT-ROW 8: Purl to end.

Rep last 2 short-rows 1 (1, 3, 3, 3, 3) more time(s).

SHORT-ROW 9: Knit to 4 (4, 4, 5, 5, 5) sts before wrapped st, wrap next st, turn.

SHORT-ROW 10: Purl to end.

Rep last 2 short-rows 0 (0, 0, 0, 0, 1) more time—depending on your size, last wrapped st is either the edge st or the st next to it.

NEXT ROW: (RS) Knit to end, working wraps tog with wrapped sts.

NEXT ROW: Purl—armhole measures 6½" (16.5 cm) above last sleeve CO.

Place sts on holder. Break yarn.

FINISHING

Block pieces to measurements. Sew side and underarm seams.

Turn piece inside out. Place 37 (41, 45, 49, 53, 57) held sts of both front shoulders on smaller cir needle, place 106 (114, 122, 126, 134, 142) held back sts on larger cir needle, and hold front and back sts tog.

Using tip of larger cir as working needle, join 37 (41, 45, 49, 53, 57) shoulder sts using three-needle BO, then BO center 32 (32, 32, 28, 28, 28) back sts, then join 37 (41, 45, 49, 53, 57) rem shoulder sts.

ARMHOLE EDGINGS

With dpn and RS facing, beg at base of armhole, pick up and knit 52 sts along armhole edge (about 4 sts for every 5 rows). Pm and join in the rnd.

Purl 1 rnd.

BO all sts kwise.

FRONT BAND

With smaller cir needle and RS facing, beg at lower right front corner, pick up and knit 92 (92, 94, 94, 96, 98) sts along right front to shoulder join, 34 (34, 34, 30, 30, 30) sts across back neck, and 92 (92, 94, 94, 96, 98) sts along left front to lower left front corner—218 (218, 222, 218, 222, 226) sts.

Beg with WS Row 2, work in Broken Rib patt until band measures 5" (12.5 cm).

BO all sts in patt. Weave in ends.

MONTEREY

TEE

Kate Gagnon Osborn

The Monterey Tee features a beautiful allover twisted-rib lace motif; the simple construction allows you to focus on the rhythmic pattern. Style this top with a simple camisole or layer it over long sleeves for transitional seasons. This tee is worked from the bottom up in pieces and then blocked to allow the openwork to bloom.

FINISHED SIZE

31¾ (37¼, 42¾, 48¼, 54¼, 59¾)" (80.5 [94.5, 108.5, 122.5, 138, 152] cm) bust circumference. Top shown measures 42¾" (108.5 cm); modeled with 8¾" (22 cm) of positive ease.

YARN

DK weight (#3)

The Fibre Co. Luma (50% merino wool, 25% organic cotton, 15% linen, 10% silk; 137 yd [125 m]/1¾ oz [50 g]): willow, 4 (5, 6, 7, 7, 8) skeins. Yarn distributed by Kelbourne Woolens.

NEEDLES

Size U.S. 4 (3.5 mm): straight and 16" circular (cir).

Size U.S. 5 (3.75 mm): straight.

Adjust needle size if necessary to obtain the correct gauge.

NOTIONS

Marker (m); removable m; stitch holders; tapestry needle.

GAUGE

20 sts and 27 rows = 4" (10 cm) in lace patt on larger needles.

NOTES

- This top is worked in pieces from the bottom up and seamed.

- During shoulder shaping, if there are not enough stitches to work a decrease with its companion yarnover or a double decrease with both its yarnovers, work the remaining stitch(es) in stockinette instead.

STITCH GUIDE

TWISTED RIB:
(EVEN NUMBER OF STS)

ROW 1: (RS) K1, *k1tbl, p1; rep from * to last st, k1.

ROW 2: (WS) P1, *k1, p1tbl; rep from * to last st, p1.

Rep Rows 1 and 2 for patt.

INSTRUCTIONS

FRONT

With smaller straight needles, CO 80 (94, 108, 122, 136, 150) sts. Work in Twisted Rib (see Stitch Guide) for 2¾" (7 cm), ending with a WS row.

Change to larger needles. Work Chart A until piece measures 15½" (39.5 cm) from CO.

Place removable m (prm) at each end of row to mark beg of armhole.

Work until armhole measures 8¼ (8¾, 9, 9, 9¼, 9½)" (21 [22, 23, 23, 23.5, 24] cm) above m, ending with a WS row.

Shape shoulders using short-rows as foll (see Notes):

SHORT-ROWS 1 AND 2: Work in patt to last 5 (6, 9, 12, 13, 16) sts, wrap next st, turn.

SHORT-ROWS 3 AND 4: Work to 4 (7, 9, 11, 14, 16) sts before wrapped st, wrap next st, turn.

SHORT-ROWS 5 AND 6: Rep Short-rows 3 and 4.

NEXT ROW: (RS) Work to end, working wraps on right shoulder tog with wrapped sts.

Place sts on holder. Do not break yarn.

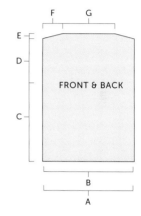

A: (Front) 16 (18¾, 21½, 24¼, 27¼, 30)" (40.5 [47.5, 54.5, 61.5, 69, 76] cm)

B: (Back) 15¾ (18½, 21¼, 24, 27, 29¾)" (40 [47, 54, 61, 68.5, 75.5] cm)

C: 15½" (39.5 cm)

D: 8¼ (8¾, 9, 9, 9¼, 9½)" (21 [22, 23, 23, 23.5, 24] cm)

E: 1" (2.5 cm)

F: 2½ (4, 5½, 6¾, 8¼, 9½)" (6.5 [10, 14, 17, 21, 24] cm)

G: 10½" (26.5 cm)

CHART A

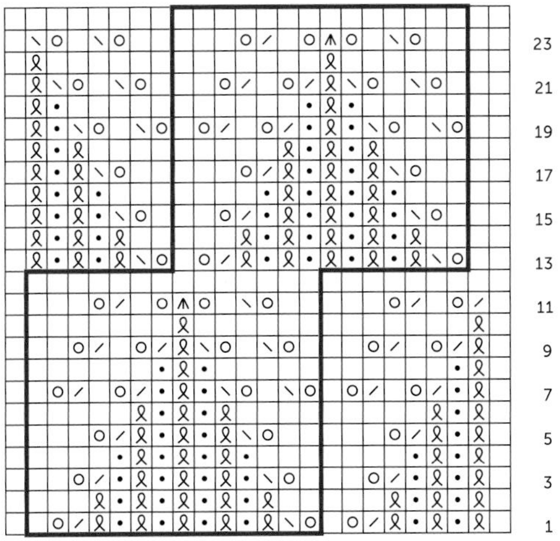

Legend:
- k on RS; p on WS
- • p on RS; k on WS
- ᛘ k1tbl on RS; p1tbl on WS
- O yo
- ╱ k2tog
- ╲ ssk
- ∧ sl 2 as if to k2tog, k1, p2sso
- M M1
- pattern repeat

Chart A row numbers: 23, 21, 19, 17, 15, 13, 11, 9, 7, 5, 3, 1

CHART B

Chart B row numbers: 23, 21, 19, 17, 15, 13, 11, 9, 7, 5, 3, 1

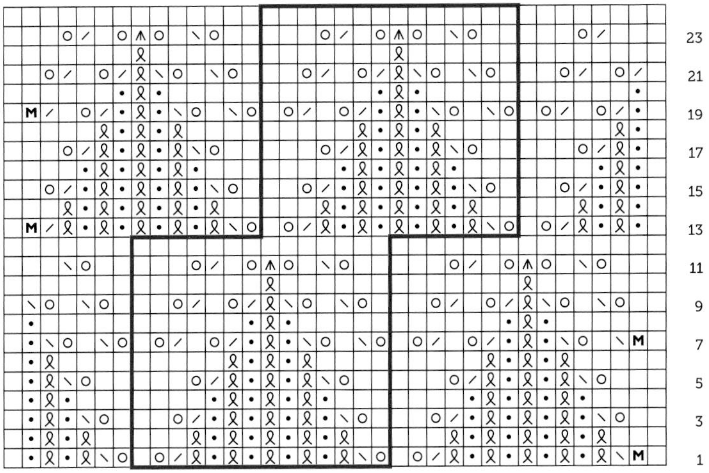

14-st rep

BACK

With smaller straight needles, CO 78 (92, 106, 120, 134, 148) sts.

Work in Twisted Rib for 2¾" (7 cm), ending with a WS row.

Change to larger needles. Work Chart B until piece measures 15½" (39.5 cm) from CO.

Pm at each end of row to mark beg of armhole.

Work until armhole measures 8¼ (8¾, 9, 9, 9¼, 9½)" (21 [22, 23, 23, 23.5, 24] cm) above m, ending with a WS row.

Shape shoulders by working Short-rows 1–6 as for front.

NEXT ROW: (RS) Work to end, working wraps on left shoulder tog with wrapped sts.

Place sts on holder. Break yarn, leaving an 80" (203 cm) tail.

FINISHING

Block to measurements.

Join shoulders using three-needle BO as foll:

Place 13 (20, 27, 34, 41, 48) left front and back shoulder sts on separate smaller needles.

Turn work inside out. Hold front and back tog with RS tog. With larger needle and using 80" (203 cm) tail attached to back, use the three-needle BO method to join left shoulder sts, hiding rem wraps as you come to them, then return st on right needle after last BO to needle holding back sts.

Place 13 (20, 27, 34, 41, 48) right front and back shoulder sts on separate smaller needles and use larger needle and yarn attached to ball to join right shoulder sts, hiding rem wraps as you come to them, then return st on right needle after last BO to needle holding front sts—106 sts rem: 54 front sts and 52 back sts.

Turn sweater RS out.

NECKBAND

Using yarn attached to ball and cir needle, beg with back sts, [k1tbl, p1] 25 times, k1tbl, ssp (last back st tog with first front st), [k1tbl, p1] 25 times, k1tbl, ssp—104 sts rem.

Place marker (pm) and join in the rnd.

NEXT RND: *K1tbl, p1; rep from * to end.

Loosely BO all sts in patt.

ARMHOLE BANDS

Sew side seams from CO edge to underarm m.

With cir needle and RS facing, beg at underarm, pick up and knit 84 (86, 90, 90, 92, 96) sts evenly around armhole edge.

Pm and join in the rnd.

NEXT 2 RNDS: *K1tbl, p1; rep from * to end.

Loosely BO all sts in patt. Weave in ends.

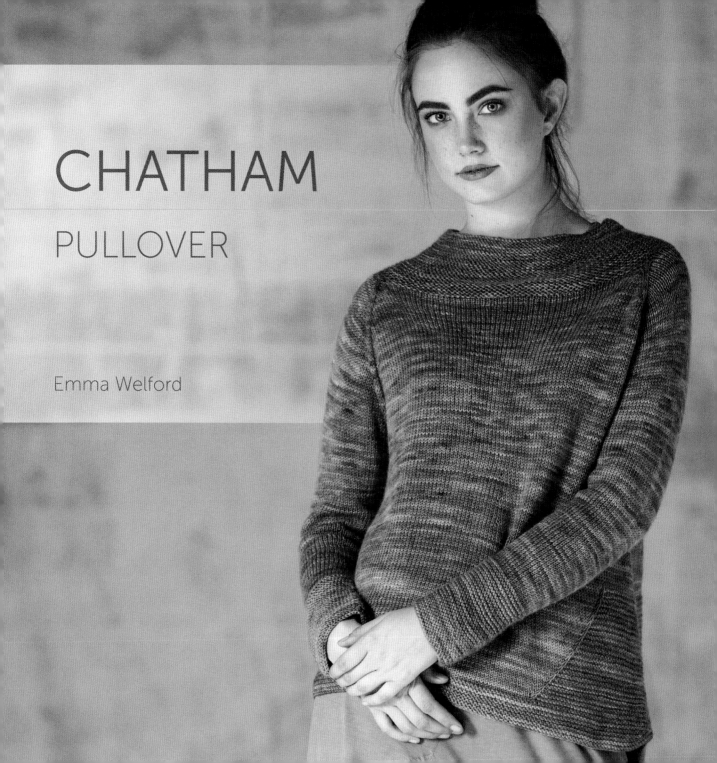

CHATHAM

PULLOVER

Emma Welford

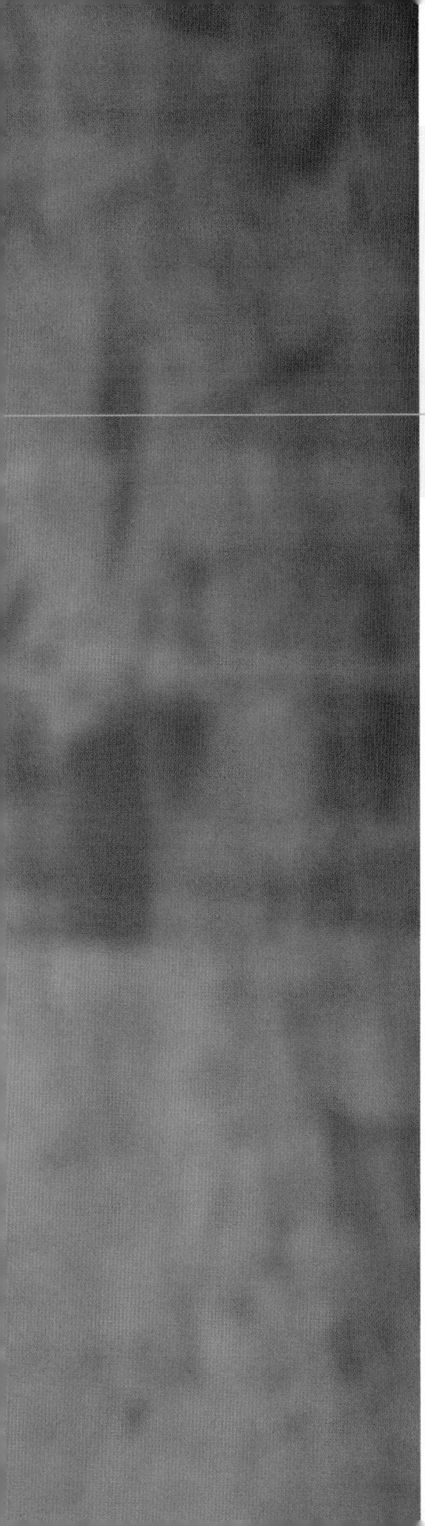

Garter stitch, stockinette, gently variegated yarn, and a mock turtle-neck make the Chatham Pullover the essential capsule wardrobe sweater. This knitter-friendly pullover is made from the top down in one piece, allowing you to work through the sweater without worrying about any fiddly finishing.

FINISHED SIZE

36½ (41¼, 45¾, 50¼, 54¾, 59½)" (92.5 [105, 116, 127.5, 139, 151] cm) bust circumference. Pullover shown measures 41¼" (92.5 cm); modeled with 6¼" (16 cm) of positive ease.

YARN

DK weight (#3)

SHOWN HERE: Mrs. Crosby Hat Box (75% superwash merino, 15% silk, 10% cashmere; 317 yd [290 m]/3½ oz [100 g]): squid ink, 4 (5, 5, 6, 7, 7) skeins.

NEEDLES

Size U.S. 5 (3.75 mm): 24" circular (cir) and set of double-pointed (dpn).

Adjust needle size if necessary to obtain the correct gauge.

NOTIONS

Markers (m); cable needle (cn); stitch holders; tapestry needle.

GAUGE

21 sts and 32 rnds = 4" (10 cm) in St st.

NOTES

- This pullover is worked in the round from the top down.

YOKE

COLLAR: With cir needle, CO 106 (114, 122, 138, 146, 154) sts. Place marker (pm) and join in the rnd.

Work in garter st (knit 1 rnd, purl 1 rnd) until piece measures 4" (10 cm) from CO.

NEXT RND: *K40 (44, 48, 54, 58, 62), pm, k2, pm, k9 (9, 9, 11, 11, 11), pm, k2, pm; rep from * once more, using rnd m as last m—40 (44, 48, 54, 58, 62) sts each for front and back, 9 (9, 9, 11, 11, 11) sts each sleeve, and 8 raglan sts in four marked 2-st lines.

SHAPE RAGLAN ARMHOLES

INC RND: *M1L, knit to m, M1R, sl m, k2, sl m; rep from * 3 more times—8 sts inc'd; 2 sts each for front and back, 2 sts each sleeve.

Working in St st, rep inc rnd every rnd 9 (12, 16, 19, 23, 29) more times, then every other rnd 15 (16, 16, 16, 16, 14) times—306 (346, 386, 426, 466, 506) sts: 90 (102, 114, 126, 138, 150) sts each for front and back, 59 (67, 75, 83, 91, 99) sts each sleeve, and 8 raglan sts.

Work even until armhole measures 7 (7½, 8, 8½, 9, 9½)" (18 [19, 20.5, 21.5, 23, 24] cm) from first raglan inc rnd.

DIVIDE FOR SLEEVES AND BODY

NEXT RND: *Knit to m, remove m, place 2 sts on holder, remove m, place next 59 (67, 75, 83, 91, 99) sleeve sts on holder, remove m, place 2 sts on holder, remove m*, then using the backward-loop method, CO 6 underarm sts; rep from * to * once more, CO 3 underarm sts, pm for new beg of rnd at right side "seam," CO 3 underarm sts—192 (216, 240, 264, 288, 312) body sts.

BODY

Work even until piece measures 3½" (9 cm) from underarm.

SET-UP RND: [K24 (27, 30, 33, 36, 39), pm] 7 times, knit to end.

INC RND: [Knit to m, M1L, sl m] 8 times—8 sts inc'd.

Rep inc rnd every 8th rnd 2 more times, removing all m on last rnd—216 (240, 264, 288, 312, 336) sts.

NEXT RND: K54 (60, 66, 72, 78, 84), pm for new beg of rnd at center front, knit to end.

Work even until piece measures 7½ (7½, 7¾, 7¾, 8, 8)" (19 [19, 19.5, 19.5, 20.5, 20.4] cm) from underarm.

SET-UP RND: K42 (44, 46, 48, 50, 52), pm, k1, p130 (150, 170, 190, 210, 230), k1, pm, k42 (44, 46, 48, 50, 52).

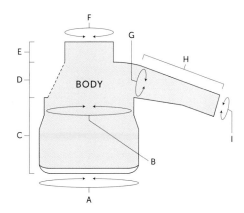

A: 41¼ (45¾, 50¼, 54¾, 59½, 64)"
(105 [116, 127.5, 139, 151, 162.5] cm)

B: 36½ (41¼, 45¾, 50¼, 54¾, 59½)"
(92.5 [105, 116, 127.5, 139, 151] cm)

C: 15 (15, 15¼, 15¼, 15½, 15½)"
(38 [38, 38.5, 38.5, 39.5, 39.5] cm)

D: 7 (7½, 8, 8½, 9, 9½)"
(18 [19, 20.5, 21.5, 23, 24] cm)

E: 4" (10 cm)

F: 20¼ (21¾, 23¼, 26¼, 27¾, 29¼)"
(51.5 [55, 59, 66.5, 70.5, 74.5] cm)

G: 13¼ (14¾, 16¼, 17¾, 19¼, 20¾)"
(33.5 [37.5, 41.5, 45, 49, 52.5] cm)

H: 17½" (44.5 cm)

I: 8½ (9¼, 9¾, 10½, 10¾, 11½)"
(21.5 [23.5, 25, 26.5, 27.5, 29] cm)

NEXT RND: Knit to m, sl m, sl 1 pwise wyb, knit to 1 st before m, sl 1 pwise wyb, sl m, knit to end.

NEXT RND: Knit to 1 st before m, pm, sl 1 st onto cn, hold in back, remove m, k1, p1 from cn, purl to 1 st before m, sl 1 st onto cn, hold in front, remove m, p1, k1 from cn, pm, knit to end.

Rep last 2 rnds 23 more times—marked section contains 178 (198, 218, 238, 258, 278) garter sts with 1 slipped st at each side; 36 (40, 44, 48, 52, 56) knit sts at center front.

NEXT RND: Knit to m, sl m, sl 1 pwise wyb, knit to 1 st before m, sl 1 pwise wyb, sl m, knit to end—piece measures about 13¾ (13¾, 14, 14, 14¼, 14¼)" (35 [35, 35.5, 35.5, 36, 36] cm) from underarm. Break yarn.

With RS facing and without working any sts, sl 18 (20, 22, 24, 26, 28) front sts pwise, remove m, sl 36 (40, 44, 48, 52, 56) sts pwise to end at left side. Rejoin yarn with WS facing.

Shape front hem using short-rows as foll:

NOTE: *Do not work wraps tog with wrapped sts.*

SHORT-ROW 1: (WS) K72 (80, 88, 96, 104, 112), remove m, k34 (38, 42, 46, 50, 54), wrap next st, turn.

SHORT-ROW 2: (RS) K104 (116, 128, 140, 152, 164), wrap next st, turn.

SHORT-ROW 3: Knit to 2 sts before wrapped st, wrap next st, turn.

SHORT-ROWS 4–8: Rep Short-row 3 five times.

SHORT-ROW 9: (WS) K100 (112, 124, 136, 148, 160) to end at right side, do not turn.

Shape back hem using short-rows as foll:

SHORT-ROW 1: (WS) K106 (118, 130, 142, 154, 166), wrap next st, turn.

SHORT-ROW 2: (RS) K104 (116, 128, 140, 152, 164), wrap next st, turn.

SHORT-ROW 3: Knit to 2 sts before wrapped st, wrap next st, turn.

SHORT-ROWS 4–14: Rep Short-row 3 eleven times.

SHORT-ROW 15: (WS) K94 (106, 118, 130, 142, 154) to end at left side, turn.

NEXT RND: Pm for new end of rnd, knit 1 entire rnd.

Purl 1 rnd, knit 1 rnd, purl 1 rnd—piece measures about 15 (15, 15¼, 15¼, 15½, 15½)" (38 [38, 38.5, 38.5, 39.5, 39.5] cm) from underarm at center back, and 1" (2.5 cm) less at center front.

Loosely BO all sts.

SLEEVES

With dpn and RS facing, beg at center of underarm, pick up and knit 3 sts from underarm CO, k63 (71, 79, 87, 95, 103) sleeve sts from holder, pick up and knit 3 sts from underarm CO—69 (77, 85, 93, 101, 109) sts.

Pm and join in the rnd.

Knit 1 rnd.

DEC RND: K1, k2tog, knit to last 3 sts, ssk, k1—2 sts dec'd. Rep dec rnd every 6th (5th, 4th, 4th, 3rd, 3rd) rnd 11 (13, 16, 18, 21, 23) more times—45 (49, 51, 55, 57, 61) sts rem.

Work even until piece measures 12½" (31.5 cm) from underarm. Work in garter st for 5" (12.5 cm). Loosely BO all sts.

FINISHING

Weave in ends. Block to measurements.

PISMO BEACH

PULLOVER

Amanda Scheuzger

The Pismo Beach Pullover showcases lightweight fibers, simple lace, easy finishing, and knitter-friendly construction. The hem of this pullover is worked flat in two pieces with the yarn held double, then the pieces are joined and one strand of yarn is broken. The rest of the body is worked in the round to the underarm using a single strand of yarn.

FINISHED SIZE

34¾ (37¾, 40½, 43½, 46¼, 50¼)" (88.5 [96, 103, 110.5, 117.5, 127.5] cm) bust circumference. Pullover shown measures 37¾" (96 cm); modeled with 3¾" (9.5 cm) of positive ease.

YARN

Fine (#2)

SHOWN HERE: Plymouth Yarn Linaza (50% alpaca, 25% linen, 25% Tencel; 440 yd [402 m]/3½ oz [100 g]): #4888 taupe, 3 (3, 4, 4, 4, 5) skeins.

NEEDLES

Size U.S. 5 (3.75 mm): 32" circular (cir) and set of double-pointed (dpn).

Adjust needle size if necessary to obtain the correct gauge.

NOTIONS

Markers (m); stitch holders; tapestry needle.

GAUGE

27 sts and 34 rows = 4" (10 cm) in St st; 7 sts of lace panel = 1¼" (3.2 cm).

NOTES

- The hem of this pullover is worked flat in two pieces with the yarn held double, then the pieces are joined and one strand of yarn is broken. The rest of the body is worked using a single strand of yarn in the round to the underarm, then the front and back are worked separately back and forth. Sts for the sleeves are picked up around the armholes, and the sleeves are worked in the round from the top down.

- During shaping, if there are not enough sts to work each dec with its companion yo, work the rem st in stockinette st instead.

- The Lace chart is worked both in rnds and back and forth in rows. When working in rnds, work every row as a RS row.

INSTRUCTIONS

BODY

FRONT HEM

With cir needle and yarn held double (see Notes), CO 71 (81, 89, 97, 103, 113) sts. Do not join.

NEXT ROW: (WS) Sl 1 pwise wyf, *p1tbl, k1; rep from * to last 2 sts, p1tbl, p1.

NEXT ROW: (RS) Sl 1 pwise wyb, *k1tbl, p1; rep from * to last 2 sts, k1tbl, k1.

Rep last 2 rows until piece measures 1½" (3.8 cm) from CO, ending with a WS row.

Place sts on holder. Break both strands and set aside.

BACK HEM

With cir needle and yarn held double, CO 149 (155, 167, 175, 189, 203) sts. Do not join.

Work as for front hem until piece measures 3" (7.5 cm) from CO, ending with a WS row.

JOIN HEMS

NEXT ROW: (RS) Using yarn held double, work across back hem sts in established patt to last st, purl last st of back hem tog with first st of front hem, work across front hem sts in established patt to last st, purl last st of front hem tog with first st of back hem—218 (234, 254, 270, 290, 314) sts.

Break 1 strand of yarn and cont working with a single strand.

NEXT RND: K19 (18, 19, 19, 21, 22), place marker (pm) for beg of rnd at right side.

NEXT RND: Knit.

NEXT RND: *K11 (7, 12, 8, 13, 11), [work Lace chart over 7 sts, k9] 5 (6, 6, 7, 7, 8) times, work Lace chart over 7 sts, k11 (7, 12, 8, 13, 11); rep from * once more.

Cont in patt as established until piece measures 19" (48.5 cm) from CO at back hem, ending with an even-numbered chart rnd.

DIVIDE FOR FRONT AND BACK

NEXT RND: Work 109 (117, 127, 135, 145, 157) back sts in patt, place next 109 (117, 127, 135, 145, 157) sts on holder for front—109 (117, 127, 135, 145, 157) sts rem for back.

Beg working back and forth in rows.

BACK

Work even until armhole measures 7 (7½, 8, 8¼, 8¾, 9¼)" (18 [19, 20.5, 21, 22, 23.5] cm), ending with a WS row.

SHAPE NECK

NEXT ROW: (RS) Work 36 (39, 44, 45, 50, 54) sts and place these sts on holder for right shoulder, BO 37 (39, 39, 45, 45, 49) sts, work in patt to end—36 (39, 44, 45, 50, 54) sts rem for left shoulder.

LEFT SHOULDER

Work 1 WS row even.

DEC ROW: (RS) Ssk, k1, work in patt to end—1 st dec'd.

Rep dec row every RS row 2 more times—33 (36, 41, 42, 47, 51) sts rem.

Work even until armhole measures 8 (8½, 9, 9¼, 9¾, 10¼)" (20.5 [21.5, 23, 23.5, 26] cm), ending with a WS row. BO all sts.

RIGHT SHOULDER

Return 36 (39, 44, 45, 50, 54) right shoulder sts to needle and, with WS facing, rejoin yarn.

Work 1 WS row even.

DEC ROW: (RS) Work in patt to last 3 sts, k1, k2tog—1 st dec'd.

Rep dec row every RS row 2 more times—33 (36, 41, 42, 47, 51) sts rem. Work even until armhole measures 8 (8½, 9, 9¼, 9¾, 10¼)" (20.5 [21.5, 23, 23.5, 26] cm), ending with a WS row. BO all sts.

FRONT

Return 109 (117, 127, 135, 145, 157) front sts to needle and, with RS facing, rejoin yarn. Work even until armhole measures 5 (5½, 6, 6¼, 6¾, 7¼)" (12.5 [14, 15, 16, 17, 18.5] cm), ending with a WS row.

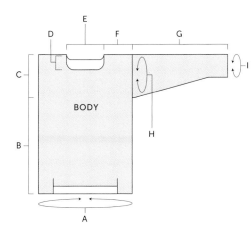

A: 34¾ (37¾, 40½, 43½, 46¼, 50¼)" (88.5 [96, 103, 110.5, 117.5, 127.5] cm)

B: 19" (48.5 cm)

C: 8 (8½, 9, 9¼, 9¾, 10¼)" (20.5 [21.5, 23, 23.5, 25, 26] cm)

D: 3" (7.5 cm)

E: 6¾ (7¼, 7¼, 8¼, 8¼, 8¾)" (17 [18.5, 18.5, 21, 21, 22] cm)

F: 5¼ (5¾, 6½, 6¾, 7½, 8¼)" (13.5 [14.5, 16.5, 17, 29, 21] cm)

G: 19" (48.5 cm)

H: 16 (16¾, 18, 18¼, 19½, 20¼)" (40.5 [42.5, 45.5, 46.5, 49.5, 51.5] cm)

I: 8¼ (8¼, 8¾, 8¾, 9½, 9½)" (21 [21, 22, 22, 24, 24] cm)

SHAPE NECK

NEXT ROW: (RS) Work 40 (43, 48, 49, 54, 58) sts and place these sts on holder for left shoulder, BO 29 (31, 31, 37, 37, 41) sts, work in patt to end—40 (43, 48, 49, 54, 58) sts rem for right shoulder.

RIGHT SHOULDER

Work 1 WS row even.

DEC ROW: (RS) Ssk, k1, work in patt to end—1 st dec'd.

Rep dec row every RS row 6 more times—33 (36, 41, 42, 47, 51) sts rem.

Work even until armhole measures 8 (8½, 9, 9¼, 9¾, 10¼)" (20.5 [21.5, 23, 23.5, 25, 26] cm), ending with a WS row. BO all sts.

LEFT SHOULDER

Return 40 (43, 48, 49, 54, 58) left shoulder sts to needle and, with WS facing, rejoin yarn.

Work 1 WS row even.

DEC ROW: (RS) Work in patt to last 3 sts, k1, k2tog—1 st dec'd.

Rep dec row every RS row 6 more times—33 (36, 41, 42, 47, 51) sts rem.

Work even until armhole measures 8 (8½, 9, 9¼, 9¾, 10¼)" (20.5 [21.5, 23, 23.5, 25, 26] cm), ending with a WS row. BO all sts.

Sew shoulder seams.

SLEEVES

With dpn and RS facing, beg at center of underarm, pick up and knit 103 (109, 117, 119, 127, 133) sts evenly around armhole edge. Pm and join in the rnd. Knit 1 rnd.

NEXT RND: K32 (35, 39, 40, 44, 47), [work Lace chart over 7 sts, k9] 2 times, work Lace chart over 7 sts, knit to end.

Work 1 rnd in patt as established.

DEC RND: K1, k2tog, work in patt to last 3 sts, ssk, k1—2 sts dec'd.

Rep dec rnd every 4th (4th, 2nd, 2nd, 2nd, 2nd) rnd 25 (28, 4, 6, 10, 12) more times, then every 0 (0, 4, 4, 4, 4)th rnd 0 (0, 26, 25, 23, 24) times—51 (51, 55, 55, 59, 59) sts rem.

NEXT RND: Work in patt to last st, knit last st tog with first st of rnd, pm for new beg of rnd—50 (50, 54, 54, 58, 58) sts rem.

Work even in patt until sleeve measures 17" (43 cm) from CO. Join 2nd strand of yarn and cont with yarn held double.

NEXT RND: *P1, k1tbl; rep from * to end. Rep last rnd until ribbing measures 2" (5 cm). BO all sts.

FINISHING

Weave in ends. Block pieces to measurements.

NECKBAND

With RS of garment facing, work an attached I-cord edging as foll:

With dpn, CO 3 sts. *Do not turn, slide sts to other end of needle, k2, sl 1 kwise wyb, pick up and knit 1 st from neck edge, psso; rep from * until neck edging is complete. Graft last 3 sts to beg I-cord sts using Kitchener st.

LEFT SLEEVE

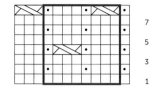

8-st rep

RIGHT SLEEVE

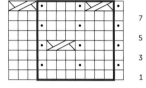

8-st rep

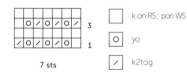

knit

purl

pattern repeat

sl 2 sts onto cn, hold in back, k1, k2 from cn

sl 1 st onto cn, hold in front, k2, k1 from cn

LACE

7 sts

k on RS; p on WS

O   yo

/   k2tog

WELLFLEET

PULLOVER

Sarah Solomon

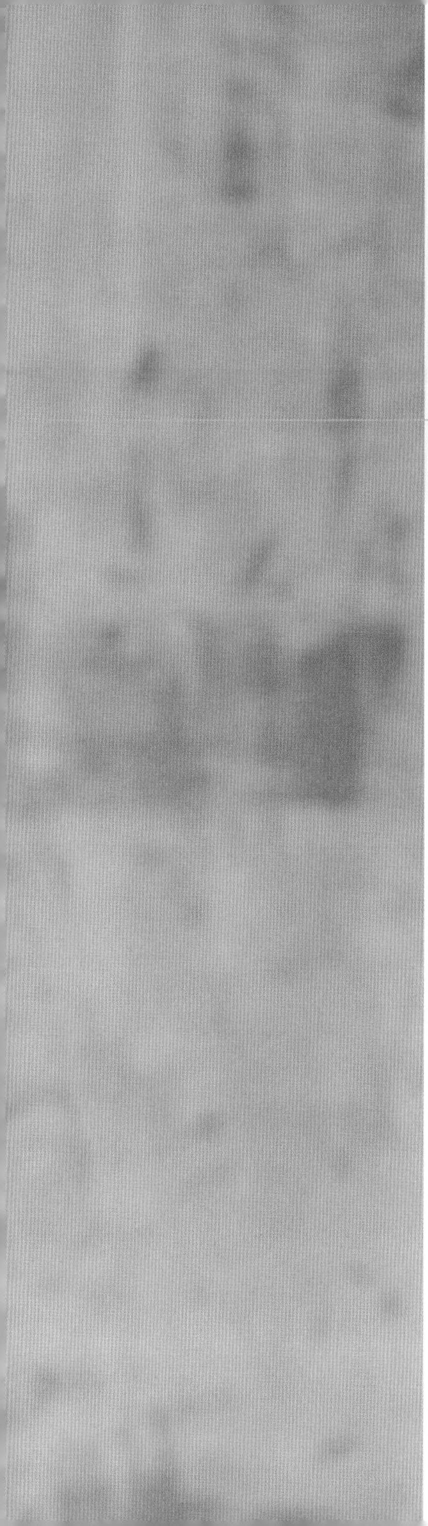

The Wellfleet Pullover is soft as a cloud, easy to wear, and a breeze to knit. The drop-shoulder construction lends visual interest to the yoke stripes; use a circular needle to avoid breaking and rejoining yarn when working a single stripe. The chainette construction of Shibui Knits Maai lets the supersoft baby alpaca/fine merino blend shine.

FINISHED SIZE

37½ (42½, 45½, 49½, 53, 57½)" (95 [108, 115.5, 125.5, 134.5, 146] cm) bust circumference. Pullover shown measures 42½" (108 cm); modeled with 8½" (21.5 cm) of positive ease.

YARN

Fingering (#1)

SHOWN HERE: Shibui Knits Maai (70% superfine baby alpaca, 30% fine merino wool; 175 yd [160 m]/1¾ oz [50 g]): #2001 abyss (MC), 7 (8, 8, 9, 10, 11) skeins; #2003 ash (CC), 1 skein.

NEEDLES

Size U.S. 5 (3.75 mm): 32" and 16" circular (cir).

Size U.S. 7 (4.5 mm): 32" cir.

Adjust needle size if necessary to obtain the correct gauge.

NOTIONS

Markers (m); removable m; stitch holder; tapestry needle.

GAUGE

20 sts and 30 rows = 4" (10 cm) in stockinette stitch on larger needle.

NOTES

- This pullover is worked back and forth in pieces and seamed.

- A circ needle is used to work the stripe pattern. To avoid breaking and rejoining yarns when working stripes with an odd number of rows, slide the sts to the end of the needle where the color needed is attached. This may require working two consecutive RS or WS rows. In the chart, arrows show the direction of knitting for each row, with red arrows indicating the "slide" rows. After completing Row 30, cut the main color (MC) and rejoin it with RS facing at the right edge of the piece, in position to work a RS row.

STITCH GUIDE

ARMHOLE INCREASES

Because of the stripe sequence, armhole increases may occur on both RS and WS rows.

WORK AN INC ROW ON A RS ROW AS FOLLOWS: K3, RLI, knit to last 3 sts, LLI, k3—2 sts inc'd.

WORK AN INC ROW ON A WS ROW AS FOLLOWS: P3, LLPI, purl to last 3 sts, RLPI, p3—2 sts inc'd.

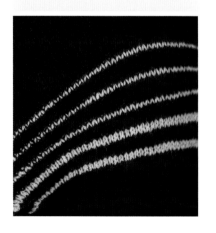

INSTRUCTIONS

BACK

With MC and smaller 32" long cir needle, using the long-tail method, CO 105 (117, 125, 135, 143, 155) sts. Do not join.

Work in k1, p1 rib for 1½" (3.8 cm), ending with a WS row.

Change to larger needle.

NEXT ROW: (RS) K2, ssk, knit to end—104 (116, 124, 134, 142, 154) sts rem.

Cont in St st until piece measures 4½" (11.5 cm) from CO, ending with a WS row.

DEC ROW: (RS) K2, ssk, knit to last 4 sts, k2tog, k2—2 sts dec'd.

Rep dec row every 20th (22nd, 22nd, 22nd, 22nd, 22nd) row 4 more times—94 (106, 114, 124, 132, 144) sts rem.

Work even until piece measures 18 (19, 19, 19, 19, 19)" (45.5 [48.5, 48.5, 48.5, 48.5, 48.5] cm) from CO, ending with a WS row.

Place a removable m at both edges of row to mark beg of armhole.

NOTE: *Armhole shaping and Stripe Sequence chart are worked simultaneously; read the foll section all the way through before proceeding.*

SHAPE ARMHOLES

Work inc row (see Notes) on next RS row, then every 4 (4, 4, 6, 6, 6)th row 6 (4, 2, 9, 7, 5) more times, then every 6 (6, 6, 0, 8, 8)th row 3 (5, 7, 0, 2, 4) times—114 (126, 134, 144, 152, 164) sts. *At the same time,* when armhole measures 1¼ (1½, 2½, 3, 3½, 4)" (3.2 [3.8, 6.5, 7.5, 9, 10] cm), ending with a WS row, beg Stripe Sequence chart.

Work through Row 30 of chart, cut MC, rejoin yarn with RS facing, then cont with MC only. When armhole shaping is complete, work even until armhole measures 6½ (7, 7¾, 8¼, 8¾, 9¼)" (16.5 [18, 19.5, 21, 22, 23.5] cm), ending with a WS row.

SHAPE SHOULDERS

BO 5 (4, 6, 7, 5, 8) sts at beg of next 4 (4, 2, 4, 2, 4) rows, then BO 4 (5, 5, 5, 6, 6) sts at beg of foll 4 (4, 6, 2, 4, 2) rows—78 (90, 92, 106, 118, 120) sts rem.

SHAPE NECK

NEXT ROW: (RS) BO 4 (5, 5, 5, 6, 6) sts, knit until there are 26 (30, 31, 38, 43, 44) sts on right needle and place these sts on holder for right shoulder, BO 18 (20, 20, 20, 20, 20) sts, knit to end—30 (35, 36, 43, 49, 50) sts rem for left shoulder.

29
27
25
23
21
19
17
15
13
11
9
7
5
3
1

→ work RS row

→ work WS row

→ with RS facing, slide sts to beg of needle, work RS row

→ with WS facing, slide sts to beg of needle, work WS row

☐ k on RS; p on WS with MC

☐ k on RS; p on WS with CC

LEFT SHOULDER

At beg of WS rows, BO 4 (5, 5, 5, 6, 6) sts 5 (5, 5, 6, 6, 6) times, and at the same time, at beg of RS rows, BO 4 sts 2 (2, 2, 1, 1, 3) time(s), then BO 2 (2, 3, 3, 3, 2) sts 1 (1, 1, 3, 3, 1) time(s)—no sts rem.

RIGHT SHOULDER

Return 26 (30, 31, 38, 43, 44) held right shoulder sts to needle and, with WS facing, rejoin yarn. At beg of WS rows, BO 4 sts 2 (2, 2, 1, 1, 3) time(s), then BO 2 (2, 3, 3, 3, 2) sts 1 (1, 1, 3, 3, 1) time(s), at the same time, at beg of RS rows, BO 4 (5, 5, 5, 6, 6) sts 4 (4, 4, 5, 5, 5) times—no sts rem.

FRONT

With MC and smaller 32" (81.5 cm) long cir needle, using the long-tail method, CO 105 (117, 125, 135, 143, 155) sts. Do not join.

Work in k1, p1 rib for ½" (1.3 cm) (1" [2.5 cm] less than back), ending with a WS row. Change to larger needle. Work as for back until piece measures 17 (18, 18, 18, 18, 18)" (43 [45.5, 45.5, 45.5, 45.5, 45.5] cm) from CO, ending with a WS row—94 (106, 114, 124, 132, 144) sts rem.

SHAPE ARMHOLES

Work inc row on next RS row, then every 4 (4, 4, 6, 6, 6)th row 2 (2, 2, 3, 4, 4) times, then every 0 (0, 6th, 0, 0, 0) row 0 (0, 1, 0, 0, 0) time, then work 1 (3, 3, 3, 1, 5) row(s) even, ending with a WS row—100 (112, 120, 132, 142, 154) sts; armhole measures 1¼ (1½, 2½, 3, 3½, 4)" (3.2 [3.8, 6.5, 7.5, 9, 10] cm).

Beg Stripe Sequence chart on next RS row, and work 30 chart rows, working shaping as foll: Work 2 (0, 2, 2, 4, 0) rows even, work inc row, rep inc row every 4 (4, 6, 6, 6, 8)th row 3 (1, 4, 4, 2, 3) time(s), then every 6 (6, 0, 0, 8, 0)th row 2 (4, 0, 0, 1, 0) time(s), then work 3 (1, 3, 3, 5, 5) row(s) even, ending with a WS row—112 (124, 130, 142, 150, 162) sts; armhole measures 5¼ (5½, 6½, 7, 7½, 8)" (13.5 [14, 16.5, 1819, 20.5] cm).

Cut MC, rejoin yarn with RS facing, then cont with MC only.

SHAPE NECK

NEXT ROW: (RS) K52 (57, 60, 65, 69, 75), BO 8 (10, 10, 12, 12, 12) sts, knit to end. Place 52 (57, 60, 65, 69, 75) left shoulder sts on holder.

RIGHT SHOULDER

NOTE: *Remaining armhole and neck shaping are worked simultaneously with the shoulder shaping; read the foll section all the way through before proceeding.*

For armhole shaping, work 1 (3, 1, 1, 1, 1) row(s) even, inc 1 st at armhole edge as established on next RS row—1 more st added at armhole edge. *At the same time,* at neck edge (beg of RS rows) BO 3 (3, 3, 4, 4, 4) sts 2 times, then BO 2 (2, 2, 2, 2, 3) sts 3 (3, 3, 3, 3, 1) time(s), then BO 0 (0, 0, 0, 0, 2) sts 0 (0, 0, 0, 0, 2) times, then BO 1 st 3 times—15 (15, 15, 17, 17, 18) sts removed at neck edge. *At the same time,* when armhole measures 6½ (7, 7¾, 8¼, 8¾, 9¼)" (16.5 [18, 19.5, 21, 22, 23.5] cm), shape shoulder as foll:

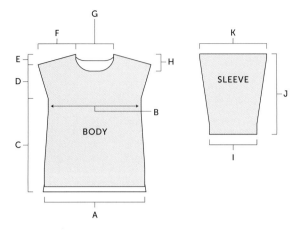

A: 20¾ (23¼, 24¾, 26¾, 28½, 30¾)"
(52.5 [59, 63, 68, 72.5, 78] cm)

B: 18¾ (21¼, 22¾, 24¾, 26½, 28¾)"
(47.5 [54, 58, 63, 67.5, 73] cm)

C: 18 (19, 19, 19, 19, 19)"
(45.5 [48.5, 48.5, 48.5, 48.5, 48.5] cm)

D: 6½ (7, 7¾, 8¼, 8¾, 9¼)"
(16.5 [18, 19.5, 21, 22, 23.5] cm)

E: 2¼" (5.5 cm)

F: 7½ (8½, 9¼, 9¾, 10½, 11½)"
(19 [21.5, 23.5, 25, 26.5, 29] cm)

G: 7½ (8, 8½, 9¼, 9¼, 9½)"
(19 [20.5, 21.5, 23.5, 23.5, 24] cm)

H: 3½ (3¾, 3½, 3½, 3½, 3½)"
(9 [9.5, 9, 9, 9, 9] cm)

I: 9½ (10½, 10¾, 11¼, 11½, 11½)"
(24 [26.5, 27.5, 28.5, 29, 29] cm)

J: 15½ (16, 16, 16, 16½, 16½)"
(39.5 [40.5, 40.5, 40.5, 42, 42] cm)

K: 13¼ (14, 15½, 16¾, 17½, 18½)"
(33.5 [35.5, 39.5, 42.5, 44.5, 47] cm)

At beg of WS rows, BO 5 (4, 6, 7, 5, 8) sts 2 (2, 1, 2, 1, 2) time(s), then BO 4 (5, 5, 5, 6, 6) sts 7 (7, 8, 7, 8, 7) times—no sts rem.

LEFT SHOULDER

Return 52 (57, 60, 65, 69, 75) held left shoulder sts to needle and, with WS facing, rejoin yarn.

NOTE: *Remaining armhole and neck shaping are worked simultaneously with the shoulder shaping; read the foll section all the way through before proceeding.*

For armhole shaping, work 1 (3, 1, 1, 1, 1) row(s) even, inc 1 st at armhole edge as established on next RS row—1 more st added at armhole edge. *At the same time*, at neck edge (beg of WS rows), BO 3 (3, 3, 4, 4, 4) sts 2 times, then BO 2 (2, 2, 2, 2, 3) sts 3 (3, 3, 3, 3, 1) time(s), then BO 0 (0, 0, 0, 0, 2) sts 0 (0, 0, 0, 0, 2) times, then BO 1 st 3 times—15 (15, 15, 17, 17, 18) sts removed at neck edge. *At the same time*, when armhole measures 6½ (7, 7¾, 8¼, 8¾, 9¼)" (16.5 [18, 19.5, 21, 22, 23.5] cm), shape shoulder as foll:

At beg of RS rows, BO 5 (4, 6, 7, 5, 8) sts 2 (2, 1, 2, 1, 2) time(s), then BO 4 (5, 5, 5, 6, 6) sts 7 (7, 8, 7, 8, 7) times—no sts rem.

SLEEVES

With MC and smaller 32" long cir needle, and using the long-tail method, CO 48 (52, 54, 56, 58, 58) sts. Do not join.

Work in k1, p1 rib until piece measures ½" (1.3 cm) from CO, ending with a WS row.

Change to larger needle and St st. Work 12 (12, 10, 8, 8, 8) rows even, ending with a WS row. Inc row (RS) K3, LLI, knit to last 3 sts, RLI, k3—2 sts inc'd.

Rep inc row every 12 (12, 10, 8, 8, 8)th row 8 (8, 4, 10, 10, 4) more times, then every 0 (0, 8, 6, 6, 6)th row 0 (0, 7, 3, 4, 12) times—66 (70, 78, 84, 88, 92) sts.

Work even until piece measures 15½ (16, 16, 16, 16½, 16½)" (39.5 [40.5, 40.5, 40.5, 42, 42] cm) from CO, ending with a WS row. BO all sts.

FINISHING

Block pieces to measurements. Sew shoulder seams.

NECKBAND

With 16" long cir needle and RS facing, beg at right shoulder seam, pick up and knit 44 (46, 48, 50, 50, 52) sts along back neck and 54 (58, 62, 66, 66, 70) sts along front neck—98 (104, 110, 116, 116, 122) sts.

Place marker (pm) and join in the rnd.

Work in k1, p1 rib for 5 rnds.

BO all sts in patt. Sew each sleeve to armhole edge, centered between armhole m, and with center of sleeve BO aligned with shoulder seam. Match last rib row of front and back at each side seam and sew seam from top of rib upwards to armhole, leaving ribbed 1½" (3.8 cm) of back and ribbed ½" (1.3 cm) of front open for side vent. Sew underarm seams from cuff to armhole.

Weave in ends.

EASTHAM

PONCHO

Mary Anne Benedetto

Is it a poncho or a cape? No matter what you call it, the Eastham Poncho is a versatile garment for every season. Worked in a neutral color, this layering piece works with jeans and a T-shirt or a graceful swirling skirt.

FINISHED SIZE

38½ (42½, 46½, 50½, 54½)" (98 [108, 118, 128.5, 138.5] cm) hip circumference. Poncho shown measures 38½" (98 cm); modeled with 2½" (6.5 cm) of positive ease.

YARN

DK weight (#3)

SHOWN HERE: Jo Sharp Alpaca Kid Lustre (40% kid mohair, 30% superfine alpaca, 30% merino; 121 yd [111 m]/1¾ oz [50 g]): #859 brew, 9 (10, 11, 12, 13) balls.

NEEDLES

Size U.S. 3 (3.25 mm): 24" circular (cir).

Size U.S. 6 (4 mm): 24" and 36" cir.

Size U.S. 5 (3.75 mm): 36" cir.

Adjust needle size if necessary to obtain the correct gauge.

NOTIONS

Markers (m); cable needle (cn); tapestry needle.

GAUGE

20 sts and 29 rnds = 4" (10 cm) in St st on largest needle.

NOTES

- The end-of-rnd marker is moved before working Rnds 5 and 7 of the Waffle Stitch chart. At the start of Rnd 5, remove the marker, sl 1 st pwise from the left needle to the right needle, replace the marker, then work the round as shown. At the start of Rnd 7, remove the marker, sl 1 st pwise from the right needle to the left needle, replace the marker, then work the rnd as shown.

- For Rnd 14 of the Waffle Panel chart, work to 1 st before the first chart marker, sl 1 st, remove the marker, return the slipped st to the left needle and work a 1/1 LT, replacing the marker in the center of the two crossed sts. Work as shown to 1 st before the second chart marker, sl 1 st, remove the marker, return the slipped st to the left needle and work a 1/1 RT, replacing the marker in the center of the two crossed sts.

STITCH GUIDE

1/1 LT

Insert needle from back to front between 1st and 2nd sts on left needle, knit 2nd st, then knit 1st st. Slip both sts off needle.

1/1 RT

Skip first st on left needle, knit 2nd st, then knit 1st st. Slip both sts off needle.

RAGLAN DETAIL (WORKED OVER 7 STS)

RND 1: K1tbl, p1tbl, k1, 1/1 LT, p1tbl, k1tbl.

RND 2: K1tbl, p1tbl, 1/1 RT, k1, p1tbl, k1tbl.

Rep Rnds 1 and 2 for patt.

INSTRUCTIONS

UPPER BODY

NECKBAND: With smaller 24" needle, and using the Old Norwegian method, CO 112 (120, 124, 128, 136) sts.

Place marker (pm) and join in the rnd.

Knit 1 rnd.

INC RND: *K1, M1P; rep from * to end—224 (240, 248, 256, 272) sts.

NEXT RND: *K1, sl 1 pwise wyf; rep from * to end.

NEXT RND: *Sl 1 pwise wyb, p1; rep from * to end.

Rep last 2 rnds 2 more times. Change to larger 24" needle.

DEC RND: *Ssk; rep from * to end—112 (120, 124, 128, 136) sts rem.

Work Rnds 1–8 of Waffle St chart once, then work Rnds 1–5 once more. Remove m, transfer 1 st from right needle to left needle without twisting it, replace m.

NEXT RND: K36 (36, 40, 44, 44), pm (right back shoulder), k20 (24, 22, 20, 24), pm (right front shoulder), k10 (10, 12, 14, 14), pm, work Waffle Panel chart over 16 sts, pm, k10 (10, 12, 14, 14), pm (left front shoulder), k20 (24, 22, 20, 24).

NOTE: *Rep Rnds 1–8 of Waffle Panel chart for patt; Rnds 9–29 will be worked later to end the panel.*

Sizes 38½ (42½)" (98 [108] cm) only

INC RND: K3, [M1, k2] 15 times, M1, k3, *sl m, k3, [M1, k2 (3)] 7 (6) times, M1, k3, sl m,* [M1, k1, M1, k2] 3 times, M1, k1, M1, sl m, work 16 sts in chart patt, sl m, [M1, k2, M1, k1] 3 times, M1, k1, M1; rep from * to * for 2nd sleeve—160 (166) sts: 52 sts each for front and back, and 28 (31) sts each sleeve.

Sizes 46½ (50½, 54½)" (118 [128.5, 138.5] cm) only

INC RND: K3 (5, 7), [M1, k2] 17 (17, 15) times, M1, k3 (5, 7), *sl m, k5 (3, 5), [M1, k2 (2, 3)] 6 (7, 5) times, M1, k5 (3, 4), sl m*, k2, [M1, k1, M1, k2] 1 (2, 1) time(s), [M1, k1] 7 (5, 6) times, k0 (1, 3), sl m, work 16 sts in chart patt, sl m, k1 (2, 2), [M1, k2, M1, k1] 1 (2, 1) time(s), [M1, k1] 7 (5, 6) times, k1 (1, 3); rep from * to * for 2nd sleeve—174 (180, 180) sts: 58 (62, 60) sts each for front and back, and 29 (28, 30) sts each sleeve.

All sizes

Without breaking yarn attached to start of back sts, transfer last 12 (14, 13, 12, 13) sts of left sleeve from right needle to left needle without working them.

Turn work so WS is facing and join new yarn. Shape left shoulder using short-rows as foll:

NOTE: *Work wraps tog with wrapped sts as you come to them.*

SHORT-ROW 1: (WS) P4, wrap next st, turn.

SHORT-ROW 2: (RS) K8, wrap next st, turn.

SHORT-ROW 3: P12, wrap next st, turn.

SHORT-ROW 4: K16, wrap next st, turn.

SHORT-ROW 5: P20, wrap next st, turn.

SHORT-ROW 6: K24, wrap next st, turn.

SHORT-ROW 7: P28. Break yarn.

With WS facing, transfer from left needle to right needle any rem left sleeve sts for your size, 52 (52, 58, 62, 60) front sts, and first 12 (14, 13, 12, 13) right sleeve sts. With WS facing, join new yarn. Work Short-rows 1–7 as for left sleeve and break short-row yarn.

Turn work so RS is facing, slide sts back to beg of rnd, and resume working with yarn attached at start of back sts.

NEXT RND: Work Raglan Detail (see Stitch Guide) over 7 sts, pm, knit to 7 sts before next m, pm, work Raglan Detail over 7 sts, *sl m, knit to next m, sl m*, work Raglan Detail over 7 sts, pm, knit to next m, sl m, work 16 sts in chart patt, sl m, knit to 7 sts before next m, pm, work Raglan Detail over 7 sts; rep from * to * once more.

Work 2 rnds even.

RAGLAN INC RND: Work 7 raglan sts, sl m, M1L, knit to next m, M1R, sl m, work 7 raglan sts, *sl m, M1L, knit to next m, M1R, sl m*, work 7 raglan sts, sl m, M1L, knit to next m, sl m, work 16 sts in chart patt, sl m, knit to next m, M1R, sl m, work 7 raglan sts; rep from * to * once more—8 sts inc'd: 2 sts each for back, front, and sleeves.

Rep raglan inc rnd every 4th (4th, 2nd, 2nd, 2nd) rnd 6 (3, 2, 10, 14) more times, then every 0 (6, 4, 4, 0)th rnd 0 (3, 6, 1, 0) time(s), changing to larger 36" needle when necessary—216 (222, 246, 276, 300) sts: 66 (66, 76, 86, 90) sts each for back and front, and 42 (45, 47, 52, 60) sts each sleeve.

Work 3 (5, 3, 3, 3) rnds even.

SLEEVE INC RND: Work 7 raglan sts, sl m, knit to next m, sl m, work 7 raglan sts, *sl m, M1L, knit to next m, M1R, sl m*, work 7 raglan sts, sl m, knit to next m, sl m, work 16 sts in chart patt, sl m, knit to next m, sl m, work 7 raglan sts; rep from * to * once more—4 sts inc'd: 2 sts each sleeve, no change to body sts.

Work 3 (5, 3, 3, 3) rnds even.

Rep raglan inc rnd—8 sts inc'd.

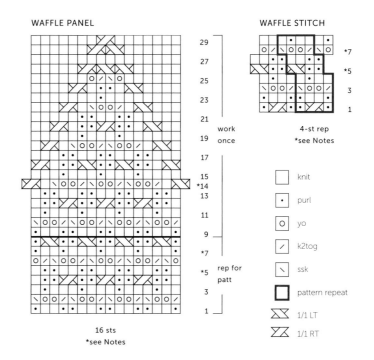

WAFFLE PANEL

WAFFLE STITCH

work once

rep for patt

16 sts
*see Notes

4-st rep
*see Notes

☐ knit
· purl
○ yo
╱ k2tog
╲ ssk
▢ pattern repeat
⧄ 1/1 LT
⧅ 1/1 RT

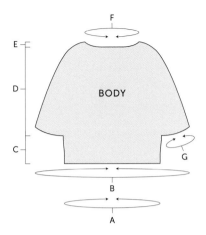

A: 38½ (42½, 46½, 50½, 54½)" (98 [108, 118, 128.5, 138.5] cm)

B: 62½ (67½, 75½, 83¼, 90½)" (159 [171.5, 191.5, 211.5, 229.5] cm)

C: 5½ (6, 6¼, 6¼, 6¼)" (14 [15, 16, 16, 16] cm)

D: 17½ (18½, 18¾, 19¼, 19¾)" (44.5 [47, 47.5, 49, 50] cm)

E: 1" (2.5 cm)

F: 21½ (23, 23¾, 24½, 26)" (54.5 [58.5, 58, 62, 66] cm)

G: 16 (16½, 18½, 20½, 22)" (40.5 [42, 47, 52, 56] cm)

Rep last 8 (12, 8, 8, 8) rnds 4 (1, 4, 6, 3) more time(s)—276 (246, 306, 360, 348) sts: 76 (70, 86, 100, 98) sts each for back and front, and 62 (53, 67, 80, 76) sts each sleeve.

NOTE: *As you work the foll shaping, cont to rep Rnds 1–8 of chart until piece measures 13½ (14¼, 14¾, 15, 15½)" (34.5 [36, 37.5, 38, 39.5] cm) from CO at center front, then work Rnds 9–29 once (see Notes), remove chart m, and work sts in St st to end.*

[Work 7 (3, 3, 3, 3) rnds even, work raglan inc rnd] 4 (10, 8, 6, 12) times—308 (326, 370, 408, 444) sts: 84 (90, 102, 112, 122) sts each for back and front, and 70 (73, 83, 92, 100) sts each sleeve.

Work 3 rnds even.

BODY INC RND: Work 7 raglan sts, sl m, M1L, knit to next m, M1R, sl m, work 7 raglan sts, *sl m, knit to next m, sl m*, work 7 raglan sts, sl m, M1L, knit to next m, sl m, work 16 sts in chart patt, sl m, knit to next m, M1R, sl m, work 7 raglan sts; rep from * to * once more—4 sts inc'd: 2 sts each for back and front, no change to sleeve sts.

Rep last 0 (4, 4, 4, 4) rnds 0 (2, 1, 1, 1) more time(s)—312 (338, 378, 416, 452) sts: 86 (96, 106, 116, 126) sts each for back and front, and 70 (73, 83, 92, 100) sleeve sts; piece measures about 17 (18, 18¼, 18¾, 19¼)" (43 [45.5, 46.5, 47.5, 49] cm) from CO at center back.

SLEEVE EDGING

NEXT RND: *Work 7 raglan sts, sl m, knit to next m, sl m, work 7 raglan sts, sl m, purl sleeve sts to next m, sl m; rep from * once more.

NEXT RND: *Work 7 raglan sts, sl m, knit to next m, sl m, work 7 raglan sts, sl m, knit sleeve sts to next m, sl m; rep from * once more.

Rep last 2 rnds once more.

DIVIDE FOR ARMHOLES

Work 7 raglan sts, sl m, *knit to next m, sl m, work 7 raglan sts, sl m, BO sleeve sts pwise until 1 sleeve st rem before next m, sl last sleeve st to right needle, BO 2nd-to-last sleeve st, remove m, return sl st to left needle, replace m, work last sleeve st tog with first raglan st as k2tog, work rem 6 raglan sts, sl m; rep from * once more—86 (96, 106, 116, 126) sts each for back and front rem; piece measures about 17½ (18½, 18¾, 19¼, 19¾)" (44.5 [47, 42.5, 49, 50] cm) from CO at center back.

LOWER BODY

NEXT RND: *Work 7 raglan sts, sl m, knit to next m, sl m, work 7 raglan sts, sl m, using the cable method, CO 10 sts, sl m; rep from * once more—192 (212, 232, 252, 272) sts: 86 (96, 106, 116, 126) sts each for back and front and 10 sts each side panel.

NEXT RND: *Work 7 raglan sts, sl m, knit to next m, sl m, work 7 raglan sts, sl m, [p2, k2] 2 times, p2, sl m; rep from * once more.

Rep last rnd 3 more times.

BODY INC AND SIDE DEC RND: *Work 7 raglan sts, sl m, M1L, knit to next m, M1R, sl m, work 7 raglan sts, sl m, k2tog, knit to 2 sts before next m, ssk, sl m; rep from * once more—2 sts each inc'd for back and front, 2 sts dec'd each side panel.

Rep body inc and side dec rnd every 10th rnd 2 more times—no change to total st count: 92 (102, 112, 122, 132) sts each for back and front and 4 sts each side panel.

Work even until lower body measures 3½ (4, 4¼, 4¼, 4¼)" (9 [10, 11, 11, 11] cm) from dividing rnd.

LOWER EDGING: [Purl 1 rnd, knit 1 rnd] 3 times. Change to smaller 36" needle. Work in k2, p2 rib until lower body measures 5½ (6, 6¼, 6¼, 6¼)" (14 [15, 16, 16, 16] cm), BO all sts using the tubular method as foll:

RND 1: *K2, sl 2 pwise wyf; rep from * to end.

RND 2: *Sl 2 pwise wyb, p2; rep from * to end.

With 2 cir needles held parallel, sl all sts as foll: *sl 2 sts to front needle, sl 2 sts to back needle; rep from * to end—same number of sts on each needle.

Break yarn, leaving a tail 4 times the length of finished edge.

With tail threaded on a tapestry needle, graft sts using Kitchener st.

FINISHING

Weave in ends. Block to measurements.

MALIBU

COWL

Susanna IC

The Malibu Cowl features a geometric lace motif that is easy to memorize for on-the-go knitting. The silky, gently tonal merino showcases the lace design and keeps your neck warm when you double up the cowl on cool summer evenings; on warmer days, wear your cowl long to show off your lace work.

FINISHED SIZE

86" (218.5 cm) circumference and 10¼" (26 cm) high.

YARN

DK weight (#3)

SHOWN HERE: Malabrigo Silky Merino (50% merino wool, 50% silk; 150 yd [137 m]/1¾ oz [50 g]): #429 Cape Cod Gray, 4 skeins.

NEEDLES

Size U.S. 7 (4.5 mm): 32" circular (cir).

Adjust needle size if necessary to obtain the correct gauge.

NOTIONS

Marker (m); tapestry needle.

GAUGE

14 sts and 31½ rnds = 4" (10 cm) in charted patt.

NOTES

* This cowl is worked circularly.

INSTRUCTIONS

COWL

Loosely CO 300 sts. Place marker (pm) and join in the rnd.

Work Rnds 1–81 of Lace chart, working rnds marked with * as foll:

RNDS 13, 53, 57, 65, 69, AND 77: Remove m, k1, pm, work chart rnd to end.

RNDS 19, 29, 33, AND 43: Remove m, transfer last st worked back to left needle, pm, work chart rnd to end.

When chart is complete, loosely BO all sts pwise.

FINISHING

Weave in ends. Lightly block piece to open up lace.

LACE

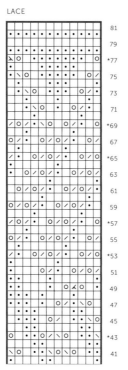

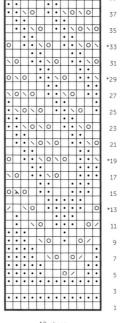

12-st rep

*Work as given in instructions

	knit
•	purl
O	yo
/	k2tog
\	ssk
⋏	k3tog
⅄	sssk
	pattern repeat

PACIFIC GROVE

TEE

Sarah Solomon

The Pacific Grove Tee is the perfect blend of simplicity and luxury. This wardrobe basic uses a lofty blended cashmere at a gauge that gives the fabric drape and allows it to breathe during the warmer months. The armhole depth is one inch longer in the front than the back, so the shoulder seam sits back from the natural shoulder.

FINISHED SIZE

39 (42½, 45½, 49, 52)" (99 [108, 115.5, 124.5, 132] cm) bust circumference. Pullover shown measures 42½" (108 cm); modeled with 8½" (21.5 cm) of positive ease.

YARN

Worsted weight (#4)

SHOWN HERE: Schoppel Wolle Cashmere Queen (45% merino wool, 35% cashmere, 20% silk; 153 yd [140 m]/1¾ oz [50 g]): #6165 parsley, 7 (7, 8, 9, 10) balls. Yarn distributed by Skacel.

NEEDLES

Size U.S. 6 (4 mm): straight and 16" circular (cir).

Size U.S. 7 (4.5 mm): straight.

Adjust needle size if necessary to obtain the correct gauge.

NOTIONS

Marker (m); removable m; stitch holders; tapestry needle.

GAUGE

20 sts and 28 rows = 4" (10 cm) in St st on larger needles.

NOTES

- This pullover is worked back and forth in separate pieces and seamed.

- The front armholes are 1" (2.5 cm) deeper than the back armholes, which moves the shoulder seam slightly behind the natural shoulder line.

- Keep 1 st at each edge in garter st for selvedge.

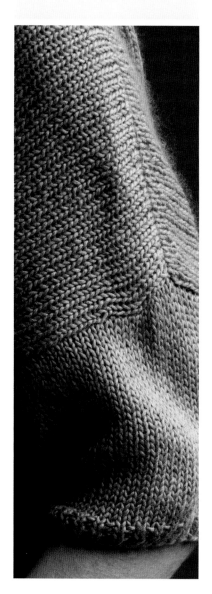

BACK

With smaller straight needles and using the long-tail method, CO 98 (106, 114, 122, 130) sts.

NEXT ROW: K1, *k1, p1; rep from * to last st, k1.

Rep last row until piece measures ¾" (2 cm) from CO, ending with a WS row.

Change to larger needles. Work in St st, keeping 1 st at each edge in garter st, until piece measures 14½ (15¼, 15¼, 15½, 15½)" (37 [38.5, 38.5, 39.5, 39.5] cm) from CO, ending with a WS row.

SHAPE ARMHOLES

Place removable m at each end of row to mark beg of armhole.

INC ROW: (RS) K3, RLI, knit to last 3 sts, LLI, k3—2 sts inc'd.

Rep inc row every 6th row 3 more times—106 (114, 122, 130, 138) sts.

Work even until armhole measures 6 (6½, 7, 7½, 8)" (15 [16.5, 18, 19, 20.5] cm), ending with a WS row.

Shape shoulders using German short-rows as foll:

SHORT-ROW 1: (RS) Work to last 4 (3, 5, 4, 5) sts, turn.

SHORT-ROW 2: (WS) Make double st, work to last 4 (3, 5, 4, 5) sts, turn.

SHORT-ROWS 3 AND 4: Make double st, work to 3 (3, 3, 3, 4) sts before double st, turn.

Rep last 2 short-rows 5 (6, 6, 7, 1) more time(s).

Size 52" (132 cm) only

SHORT-ROWS 5 AND 6: Make double st, work to 3 sts before double st, turn.

Rep last 2 short-rows 5 more times.

All sizes

NEXT ROW: (RS) Make double st, work to end, working each double st as a single st.

NEXT ROW: (WS) Work 32 (35, 37, 40, 42) sts and place these sts on holder for left shoulder, BO 42 (44, 48, 50, 54) sts, work to end, working each double st as a single st—32 (35, 37, 40, 42) sts rem for right shoulder. Place sts on holder.

FRONT

Work as for back until armhole measures 3 (3¾, 3¾, 4½, 4½)" (7.5 [9.5, 9.5,11.5, 11.5] cm), ending with a WS row—106 (114, 122, 130, 138) sts.

SHAPE NECK

NEXT ROW: (RS) K46 (49, 51, 54, 56) and place these sts on holder for left front, BO 14 (16, 20, 22, 26) sts, knit to end—46 (49, 51, 54, 56) sts rem for right front.

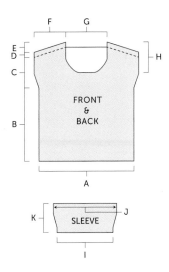

A: 19½ (21¼, 22¾, 24½, 26)"
(49.5 [54, 58, 62, 66] cm)

B: 14½ (15¼, 15¼, 15½, 15½)"
(37 [38.5, 38.5, 39.5, 39.5] cm)

C: 6 (6½, 7, 7½, 8)"
(15 [16.5, 18, 19, 20.5] cm)

D: 1" (2.5 cm)

E: 2 (2¼, 2¼, 2½, 2½)"
(5 [5.5, 5.5, 6.5, 6.5] cm)

F: 6½ (7, 7½, 8, 8½)"
(16.5 [18, 19, 20.5, 21.5] cm)

G: 8½ (8¾, 9½, 10, 10¾)"
(21.5 [22, 24, 25.5, 27.5] cm)

H: 6 (6, 6½, 6½, 7)"
(15 [15, 16.5, 16.5, 18] cm)

I: 11½ (12, 13¼, 14, 15¼)"
(29 [30.5, 33.5, 35.5, 38.5] cm)

J: 13¼ (14, 15¼, 16, 17¼)"
(33.5 [35.5, 38.5, 40.5, 44] cm)

K: 5¾ (5¾, 6¼, 6¾, 6¾)"
(14.5 [14.5, 16, 17, 17] cm)

RIGHT FRONT

Work 1 WS row.

At beg of RS rows, BO 4 sts once, then BO 3 sts once, then BO 2 sts 2 times—35 (38, 40, 43, 45) sts rem.

Work 1 WS row.

DEC ROW: (RS) Ssk, knit to end—1 st dec'd.

Rep dec row every 4th row 2 more times—32 (35, 37, 40, 42) sts rem.

Work even until armhole measures 7 (7½, 8, 8½, 9)" (18 [19, 20.5, 21.5, 23] cm), ending with a WS row.

Shape shoulder using short-rows as foll:

SHORT-ROW 1: (RS) Work to last 4 (3, 5, 4, 5) sts, turn.

SHORT-ROW 2: (WS) Make double st, work to end.

SHORT-ROW 3: Work to 3 (3, 3, 3, 4) sts before double st, turn.

SHORT-ROW 4: Make double st, work to end.

Rep last 2 short-rows 5 (6, 6, 7, 1) more time(s).

Size 52" (132 cm) only

SHORT-ROW 5: Work to 3 sts before double st, turn.

SHORT-ROW 6: Make double st, work to end.

Rep last 2 short-rows 5 more times.

All sizes

NEXT ROW: (RS) Work to end, working each double st as a single st. Place sts on holder.

LEFT FRONT

Return 46 (49, 51, 54, 56) left front sts to needle and, with WS facing, rejoin yarn.

At beg of WS rows, BO 4 sts once, then BO 3 sts once, then BO 2 sts 2 times—35 (38, 40, 43, 45) sts rem.

DEC ROW: (RS) Knit to last 2 sts, k2tog—1 st dec'd.

Rep dec row every 4th row 2 more times—32 (35, 37, 40, 42) sts rem.

Work even until armhole measures 7 (7½, 8, 8½, 9)" (18 [19, 20.5, 21.5, 23] cm), ending with a RS row.

Shape shoulder using short-rows as foll:

SHORT-ROW 1: (WS) Work to last 4 (3, 5, 4, 5) sts, turn.

SHORT-ROW 2: (RS) Make double st, work to end.

SHORT-ROW 3: Work to 3 (3, 3, 3, 4) sts before double st, turn.

SHORT-ROW 4: Make double st, work to end.

Rep last 2 short-rows 5 (6, 6, 7, 1) more time(s).

Size 52" (132 cm) only

SHORT-ROW 5: Work to 3 sts before double st, turn.

SHORT-ROW 6: Make double st, work to end.

Rep last 2 short-rows 5 more times.

All sizes

NEXT ROW: (WS) Work to end, working each double st as a single st. Place sts on holder.

SLEEVES

With smaller straight needles, CO 58 (60, 66, 70, 76) sts.

NEXT ROW: (RS) K1, *k1, p1; rep from * to last st, k1.

Rep last row until piece measures ½" (1.3 cm) from CO, ending with a WS row.

Change to larger needles and St st. Work 4 (2, 4, 4, 4) rows even.

INC ROW: (RS) K3, RLI, knit to last 3 sts, LLI, k3—2 sts inc'd. Rep inc row every 6th row 3 (4, 4, 4, 4) more times—66 (70, 76, 80, 86) sts.

Work even until piece measures 5¾ (5¾, 6¼, 6¾, 6¾)" (14.5 [14.5, 16, 17, 17] cm) from CO, ending with a WS row.

Loosely BO all sts.

FINISHING

Weave in ends. Block pieces to measurements.

With RS tog, join shoulders using three-needle BO.

NECKBAND

With cir needle and RS facing, beg at right shoulder seam, pick up and knit 42 (44, 48, 50, 54) sts along back neck and 88 (90, 96, 102, 108) sts along front neck—130 (134, 144, 152, 162) sts total.

Place marker (pm) and join in the rnd. Work in k1, p1 rib for 5 rnds.

BO all sts in patt.

Sew sleeves into armholes. Sew side seams from lower edge to under-arm. Sew sleeve seams from cuff to underarm.

BREWSTER

CARDIGAN

Linda Marveng

Alluring cables and a draped loop cowl create the unusual but captivating silhouette of the Brewster Cardigan. The generous loop cowl can double as pockets, or the extension can be omitted entirely! Either way, the stunning cables and comfortable fit will make this cardigan a favorite for years to come.

FINISHED SIZE

35 (38, 40, 44, 47½, 53½)" (89 [96.5, 101.5, 112, 120.5, 136] cm) bust circumference. Cardigan shown measures 40" (101.5 cm); modeled with 6" (15 cm) of positive ease.

YARN

DK weight (#3)

SHOWN HERE: Valley Yarns Northfield (70% merino wool, 20% baby alpaca, 10% silk; 124 yd [113 m]/1¾ oz [50 g]): #14 haze, 19 (20, 21, 23, 24, 25) skeins.

NEEDLE

Size U.S. 6 (4 mm): 16" and 32" circular (cir) and set of double-pointed (dpn).

Adjust needle size if necessary to obtain the correct gauge.

NOTIONS

Markers (m); cable needle (cn); stitch holders; tapestry needle.

GAUGE

22 sts and 30 rows = 4" (10 cm) in St st; 48 sts of Sand Cable chart = 5½" (14 cm) wide.

NOTES

- This cardigan is worked back and forth in one piece to the armholes, and then the fronts and back are worked separately. The sleeves are worked in the round, with the sleeve cap worked flat.

- A circ needle is used to accommodate the large number of sts.

- The Sand Cable chart is worked both in rnds and back and forth in rows. When working in rnds, work every chart row as a RS row.

BODY

With longer cir needle, CO 156 (176, 186, 204, 226, 258) sts. Do not join.

NEXT ROW: (RS) K30 (36, 38, 42, 48, 56), place marker (pm) for side, p1, k94 (102, 108, 118, 128, 144), p1, pm for side, k30 (36, 38, 42, 48, 56).

NEXT ROW: (WS) P1, knit to last st, p1. Rep last 2 rows 2 more times, sl m on subsequent reps.

NEXT ROW: (RS) Knit to m, sl m, p1, k17 (21, 24, 29, 34, 42), pm, *k4, [M1, k1] 6 times; rep from * 5 more times, pm, k17 (21, 24, 29, 34, 42), p1, sl m, knit to end—192 (212, 222, 240, 262, 294) sts: 30 (36, 38, 42, 48, 56) sts each front, 18 (22, 25, 30, 35, 43) right or left back sts, and 96 center back sts.

NEXT ROW: (WS) P1, k2, p25 (31, 33, 37, 43, 51), k2, sl m, k3, p13 (17, 20, 25, 30, 38), k2, sl m, *k4, [k1, p1] 2 times; rep from * 11 more times, sl m, k2, p13 (17, 20, 25, 30, 38), k3, sl m, k2, p25 (31, 33, 37, 43, 51), k2, p1.

NEXT ROW: (RS) Knit to m, sl m, p1, knit to m, sl m, work Sand Cable chart over 96 sts, sl m, knit to 1 st before m, p1, sl m, knit to end.

NEXT ROW: (WS) P1, k2, purl to 2 sts before m, k2, sl m, k3, purl to 2 sts before m, k2, sl m, work in patt to m, sl m, k2, purl to 3 sts before m, k3, sl m, k2, purl to last 3 sts, k2, p1.

Cont in patt as established until piece measures 14¼" (36 cm) from CO, ending with a WS row.

DIVIDE FOR FRONTS AND BACK

NEXT ROW: (RS) Work in patt to 4 sts before side m, BO 9 sts, removing m, work in patt to 5 sts before side m, BO 9 sts, removing m, work in patt to end—26 (32, 34, 38, 44, 52) sts rem for each front and 122 (130, 136, 146, 156, 172) back sts rem.

Place back and right front sts on holders.

LEFT FRONT

Work 1 WS row even.

SHAPE ARMHOLE: At beg of RS rows, BO 0 (0, 0, 4, 4, 4) sts once, then BO 3 sts 1 (1, 1, 1, 2, 2) time(s), then BO 2 sts 1 (2, 2, 1, 1, 3) time(s), then BO 1 st 0 (1, 1, 1, 2, 4) time(s)—21 (24, 26, 28, 30, 32) sts rem.

Sizes 38 (40, 44, 47½, 53½)" (96.5 [101.5, 112, 120.5, 136] cm) only

Work 1 WS row even.

SHAPE NECK: Dec row (RS) Knit to last 4 sts, k2tog, k2—1 st dec'd. Work 3 rows even. Rep dec row once more—22 (24, 26, 28, 30) sts rem.

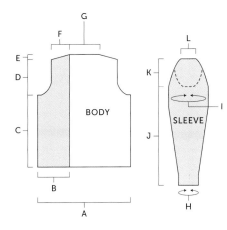

A: 17½ (19, 20, 22, 23¾, 26¾)"
(44.5 [48.5, 51, 56, 60.5, 68] cm)

B: 5½ (6½, 7, 7¾, 8¾, 10¼)"
(14 [16.5, 18, 19.5, 22, 26] cm)

C: 14¼" (36 cm)

D: 6¾ (7, 7½, 7¾, 8¼, 8¾)"
(17 [18, 19, 19.5, 21, 22] cm)

E: ¾" (2 cm)

F: 3¾ (4, 4¼, 4¾, 5, 5½)"
(9.5 [10, 11, 12, 12.5, 14] cm)

G: 6¼ (6¼, 6½, 7, 6½, 6½)"
(16 [16, 16.5, 18, 16.5, 16.5] cm)

H: 7½ (8¼, 9, 9¾, 10½, 11)"
(19 [21, 23, 25, 26.5, 28] cm)

I: 11½ (12¼, 13, 13¾, 14½, 15)"
(29 [31, 33, 35, 37, 38] cm)

J: 19¼ (19¾, 19¾, 20, 20, 20½)"
(49 [50, 50, 51, 51, 54.5] cm)

K: 5 (5¼, 5¾, 6, 6½, 6¾)"
(12.5 [13.5, 14.5, 15, 16.5, 17] cm)

L: 3 (3¼, 3¼, 3¾, 3¾, 4)"
(7.5 [8.5, 8.5, 9.5, 9.5, 10] cm)

All sizes

Work even until armhole measures 6¾ (7, 7½, 7¾, 8¼, 8¾)" (17 [18, 19, 19.5, 21, 22] cm), ending with a RS row.

Shape shoulder using short-rows as foll:

SHORT-ROW 1: (WS) Work in patt to last 7 (7, 8, 8, 9, 10) sts, wrap next st, turn.

SHORT-ROW 2: (RS) Work in patt to end.

SHORT-ROW 3: Work 7 (7, 8, 8, 9, 10) sts, wrap next st, turn.

SHORT-ROW 4: Work in patt to end.

NEXT ROW: (WS) Work in patt to end, working wraps tog with wrapped st. Place sts on holder.

RIGHT FRONT

Return 26 (32, 34, 38, 44, 52) right front sts to needle and, with WS facing, rejoin yarn.

SHAPE ARMHOLE: At beg of WS rows, BO 0 (0, 0, 4, 4, 4) sts once, then BO 3 sts 1 (1, 1, 1, 2, 2) time(s), then BO 2 sts 1 (2, 2, 1, 1, 3) time(s), then BO 1 st 0 (1, 1, 1, 2, 4) time(s)—21 (24, 26, 28, 30, 32) sts rem.

Sizes 38 (40, 44, 47½, 53½)" (96.5 [101.5, 112, 120.5, 136] cm) only

SHAPE NECK: Dec row (RS) K2, ssk, knit to end—1 st dec'd. Work 3 rows even. Rep dec row once more—22 (24, 26, 28, 30) sts rem.

All sizes

Work even until armhole measures 6¾ (7, 7½, 7¾, 8¼, 8¾)" (17 [18, 19, 19.5, 21, 22] cm), ending with a WS row. Shape shoulder using short-rows as foll:

SHORT-ROW 1: (RS) Work in patt to last 7 (7, 8, 8, 9, 10) sts, wrap next st, turn.

SHORT-ROW 2: (WS) Work in patt to end.

SHORT-ROW 3: Work 7 (7, 8, 8, 9, 10) sts, wrap next st, turn.

SHORT-ROW 4: Work in patt to end.

NEXT ROW: (RS) Work in patt to end, working wraps tog with wrapped st. Place sts on holder.

BACK

Return 122 (130, 136, 146, 156, 172) back sts to needle and, with WS facing, rejoin yarn. Work 1 WS row even.

SHAPE ARMHOLES: BO 0 (0, 0, 4, 4, 4) sts at beg of next 0 (0, 0, 2, 2, 2) rows, then BO 3 sts at beg of next 2 (2, 2, 2, 4, 4) rows, then BO 2 sts at beg of next 2 (4, 4, 2, 2, 6) rows, then BO 0 (1, 1, 1, 1, 1) st at beg of next 0 (2, 2, 2, 4, 8) rows—112 (114, 120, 126, 128, 132) sts rem.

Work even until armhole measures 6¾ (7, 7½, 7¾, 8¼, 8¾)" (17 [18, 19, 19.5, 21, 22] cm) ending with a RS row.

Gather cables

NEXT ROW: (WS) Purl to m, remove m, *work 2 sts in patt, [work 2 sts tog in patt] 6 times, work 2 sts in patt; rep from * 5 more times, remove m, purl to end—76 (78, 84, 90, 92, 96) sts rem.

NOTE: *Work all sts in St st to end.*

Shape neck and shoulders

NEXT ROW: (RS) K21 (22, 24, 26, 28, 30) sts for right shoulder, place rem 55 (56, 60, 64, 64, 66) sts on holder. Shape right shoulder using short-rows as foll:

SAND CABLE

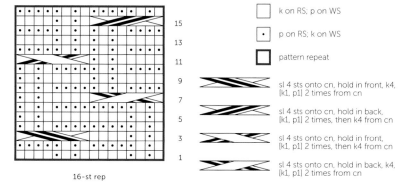

16-st rep

k on RS; p on WS

p on RS; k on WS

pattern repeat

sl 4 sts onto cn, hold in front, k4, [k1, p1] 2 times from cn

sl 4 sts onto cn, hold in back, [k1, p1] 2 times, then k4 from cn

sl 4 sts onto cn, hold in front, [k1, p1] 2 times, then k4 from cn

sl 4 sts onto cn, hold in back, k4, [k1, p1] 2 times from cn

SHORT-ROW 1: (WS) Purl to last 7 (7, 8, 8, 9, 10) sts, wrap next st, turn.

SHORT-ROW 2: (RS) Knit to end.

SHORT-ROW 3: P7 (7, 8, 8, 9, 10), wrap next st, turn.

SHORT-ROW 4: Knit to end.

NEXT ROW: (WS) Purl to end, working wraps tog with wrapped st. Place sts on holder.

Return 55 (56, 60, 64, 64, 66) sts to needle and, with RS facing, rejoin yarn.

NEXT ROW: (RS) BO 34 (34, 36, 38, 36, 36) sts, knit to end—21 (22, 24, 26, 28, 30) sts rem.

Purl 1 WS row. Shape left shoulder using short-rows foll:

SHORT-ROW 1: (RS) Knit to last 7 (7, 8, 8, 9, 10) sts, wrap next st, turn.

SHORT-ROW 2: (WS) Purl to end.

SHORT-ROW 3: K7 (7, 8, 8, 9, 10), wrap next st, turn.

SHORT-ROW 4: Purl to end.

NEXT ROW: (RS) Knit to end, working wraps tog with wrapped sts. Place sts on holder.

SLEEVES

With dpn, CO 37 (41, 45, 49, 53, 57) sts. Pm and join in the rnd.

NEXT RND: P1, knit to end.

NEXT RND: Purl.

Rep last 2 rnds once more.

NEXT RND: P1, k10 (12, 14, 16, 18, 20), pm, [k1, M1] 16 times, pm, k10 (12, 14, 16, 18, 20)—53 (57, 61, 65, 69, 73) sts.

NEXT RND: P3, k6 (8, 10, 12, 14, 16), p2, sl m, *[k1, p1] 2 times, p4; rep from * once more, sl m, p2, k6 (8, 10, 12, 14, 16), p2.

NEXT RND: P1, k10 (12, 14, 16, 18, 20), sl m, work Sand Cable chart over 32 sts, sl m, k10 (12, 14, 16, 18, 20).

NEXT RND: P3, k6 (8, 10, 12, 14, 16), p2, sl m, work in patt to m, sl m, p2, k6 (8, 10, 12, 14, 16), p2. Cont in patt as established until piece measures 2" (5 cm).

INC RND: P1, k3, M1, work in patt to last 3 sts, M1, k3—2 sts inc'd.

Rep inc rnd every 10th rnd 10 more times, working new sts into St st, and changing to 16" cir needle when necessary—75 (79, 83, 87, 91, 95) sts.

Work even until piece measures 19¼ (19¾, 19¾, 20, 20, 20½)" (49 [50, 50, 51, 51, 52] cm) from CO, ending with an even-numbered chart rnd and ending 4 sts before end of rnd on last rnd.

NEXT RND: BO 9 sts, work in patt to end—66 (70, 74, 78, 82, 86) sts rem.

Beg working back and forth in rows.

SHAPE CAP

Work 1 WS row even.

DEC ROW: (RS) K2, ssk, work in patt to last 4 sts, k2tog, k2—2 sts dec'd.

Rep dec row every 4th row 4 (4, 4, 4, 4, 3) more times, then every other row 7 (8, 10, 11, 13, 15) times—42 (44, 44, 46, 46, 48) sts rem. Work 1 (1, 1, 1, 1, 3) row(s) even.

BO 2 sts at beg of next 2 rows—38 (40, 40, 42, 42, 44) sts rem.

NEXT ROW: (RS) BO 3 sts, work to end—35 (37, 37, 39, 39, 41) sts rem.

Gather cables

NEXT ROW: (WS) BO 3 sts, work in patt to m, remove m, [work 2 sts tog in patt] 16 times, remove m, purl to end—16 (18, 18, 20, 20, 22) sts rem. BO all sts.

LOOP COLLAR

With shorter cir needle, CO 30 sts. Knit 5 rows.

NEXT ROW: (WS) K3, pm, [k1, M1] 24 times, pm, k3—54 sts.

NEXT ROW: (RS) K3, sl m, work Sand Cable chart over 48 sts, sl m, k3.

NEXT ROW: (WS) K3, sl m, work in patt to last 3, sl m, k3. Cont in patt as established until piece measures 58¼" (148 cm) from CO, ending with a RS row.

Gather cables

NEXT ROW: (WS) K3, remove m, *work 2 sts tog in patt; rep from * to last 3 sts, k3—30 sts rem.

Knit 4 rows. Place sts on holder.

Make another identical collar piece.

With WS facing, join collar pieces using three-needle BO.

FINISHING

Block to measurements, blocking loop collar rectangle to 6½" (16.5 cm) wide and 118" (300 cm) long.

Join shoulders using three-needle BO.

Sew sleeves into armholes.

With three-needle BO in center of joined collar pieces aligned with center back neck, pin collar along neck and front edges, then sew collar to body.

Sew short CO edges of collar tog to form a loop, being careful not to twist. Weave in ends.

THOUSAND OAKS

SCARF

Grace Akhrem

Covered in intermittent cables that twist like branches, the Thousand Oaks Scarf is true to its name. This luscious scarf is worked on the bias, starting with one stitch and growing with increases at either edge; short-rows add interest to this one-of-a-kind accessory. The chainette cashmere yarn adds to the decadence of this piece, making the experience of knitting and wearing this scarf equally heady.

FINISHED SIZE

12½" (31.5 cm) wide and 91" (231 cm) long.

YARN

Worsted weight (#4)

SHOWN HERE: Lana Grossa Alta Moda Cashmere 16 (78% merino wool, 12% cashmere, 10% nylon; 120 yd [110 m]/ 1¾ oz [50 g]): #001 light gray mottled, 10 skeins. Yarn distributed by Trendsetter Yarns.

NEEDLES

Size U.S. 8 (5 mm).

Adjust needle size if necessary to obtain the correct gauge.

NOTIONS

Cable needle (cn); tapestry needle.

GAUGE

16 sts and 22 rows = 4" (10 cm) in St st.

NOTES

- Work wraps together with wrapped st when you come to them.
- Only RS rows are shown on the charts. Work all WS chart rows as follows: K4, purl to last 4 sts, k4.

INSTRUCTIONS

CO 1 st.

INCREASE SECTION

ROW 1: (RS) K1fb&f—3 sts.

ROWS 2, 4, AND 6: (WS) Knit.

ROW 3: [K1f&b] 2 times, k1—5 sts.

ROW 5: K1f&b, k2, k1f&b, k1—7 sts.

ROW 7: K1f&b, k4, k1f&b, k1—9 sts.

ROW 8: K4, p1, k4.

Work Increase chart (see Notes), ending with a RS row—67 sts.

Shape corner using short-rows (see Notes) as foll:

SHORT-ROW 1: (WS) K3, wrap next st, turn.

SHORT-ROW 2: (RS) K3.

SHORT-ROW 3: K2, wrap next st, turn.

SHORT-ROW 4: K2.

SHORT-ROW 5: K1, wrap next st, turn.

SHORT-ROW 6: K1.

SHORT-ROW 7: K2, wrap next st, turn.

SHORT-ROW 8: K2.

SHORT-ROW 9: K3, wrap next st, turn.

SHORT-ROW 10: K3.

NEXT ROW: (WS) K4, purl to last 4 sts, k4.

BIAS SECTION

Work Bias 1 chart. Work Bias 2 chart. Work Bias 3 chart. Work Bias 4 chart, ending with a WS row.

Shape corner using short-rows as foll:

SHORT-ROW 1: (RS) K3, wrap next st, turn.

SHORT-ROW 2: (WS) K3.

SHORT-ROW 3: K2, wrap next st, turn.

SHORT-ROW 4: K2.

SHORT-ROW 5: K1, wrap next st, turn.

SHORT-ROW 6: K1.

SHORT-ROW 7: K2, wrap next st, turn.

SHORT-ROW 8: K2.

SHORT-ROW 9: K3, wrap next st, turn.

SHORT-ROW 10: K3.

DECREASE SECTION

Work Decrease chart, ending with a RS row—1 st rem. Fasten off last st.

FINISHING

Weave in ends. Block to measurements.

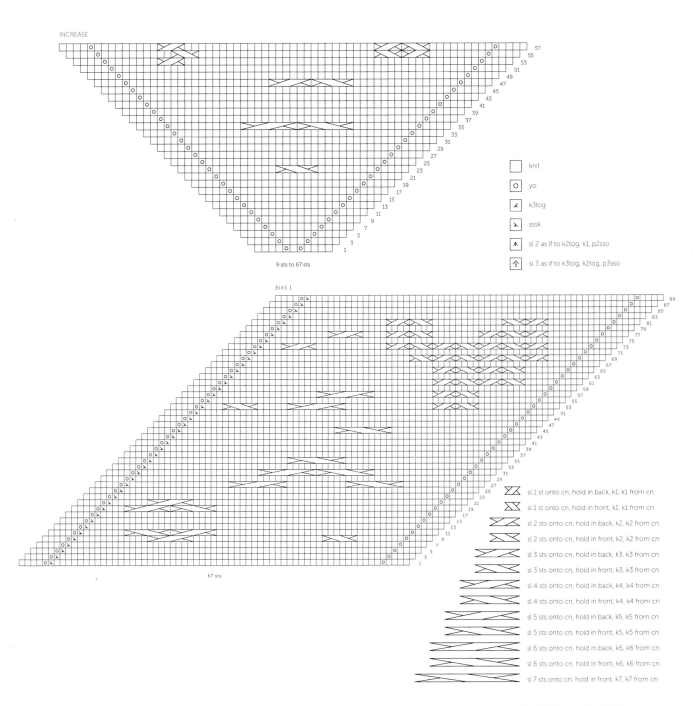

INCREASE

9 sts to 67 sts

57
55
53
51
49
47
45
43
41
39
37
35
33
31
29
27
25
23
21
19
17
15
13
11
9
7
5
3
1

	knit
O	yo
	k3tog
	sssk
Λ	sl 2 as if to k2tog, k1, p2sso
	sl 3 as if to k3tog, k2tog, p3sso

BIAS 1

67 sts

89
87
85
83
81
79
77
75
73
71
69
67
65
63
61
59
57
55
51
49
47
45
43
41
39
37
35
33
31
29
27
25
23
21
19
17
15
13
11
9
7
5
3
1

sl 1 st onto cn, hold in back, k1, k1 from cn
sl 1 st onto cn, hold in front, k1, k1 from cn
sl 2 sts onto cn, hold in back, k2, k2 from cn
sl 2 sts onto cn, hold in front, k2, k2 from cn
sl 3 sts onto cn, hold in back, k3, k3 from cn
sl 3 sts onto cn, hold in front, k3, k3 from cn
sl 4 sts onto cn, hold in back, k4, k4 from cn
sl 4 sts onto cn, hold in front, k4, k4 from cn
sl 5 sts onto cn, hold in back, k5, k5 from cn
sl 5 sts onto cn, hold in front, k5, k5 from cn
sl 6 sts onto cn, hold in back, k6, k6 from cn
sl 6 sts onto cn, hold in front, k6, k6 from cn
sl 7 sts onto cn, hold in front, k7, k7 from cn

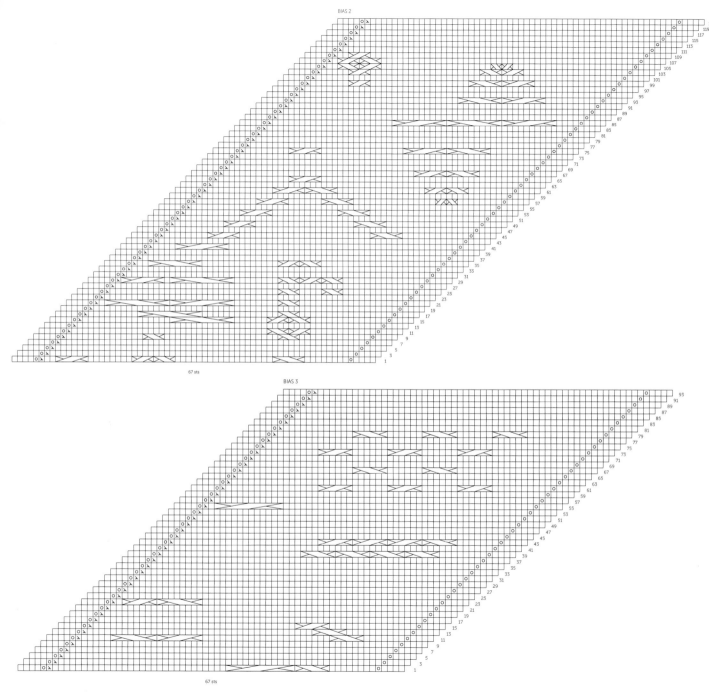

BIAS 2

67 sts

BIAS 3

67 sts

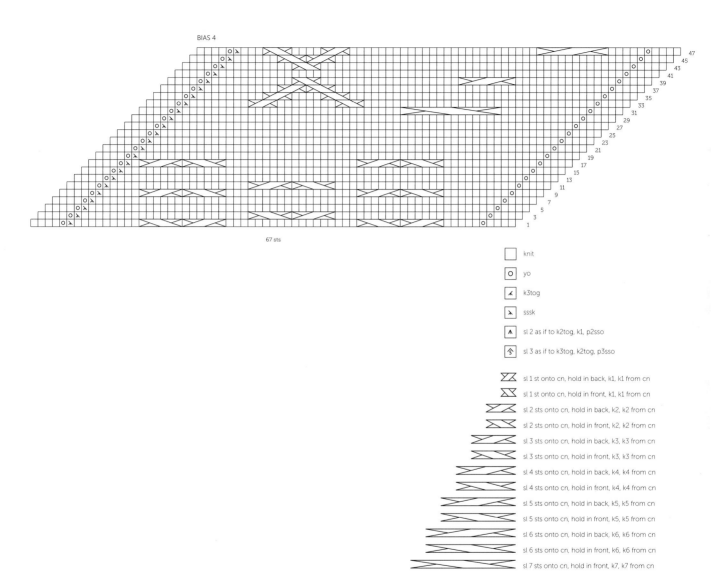

BIAS 4

67 sts

	knit
O	yo
	k3tog
	sssk
	sl 2 as if to k2tog, k1, p2sso
	sl 3 as if to k3tog, k2tog, p3sso

sl 1 st onto cn, hold in back, k1, k1 from cn
sl 1 st onto cn, hold in front, k1, k1 from cn
sl 2 sts onto cn, hold in back, k2, k2 from cn
sl 2 sts onto cn, hold in front, k2, k2 from cn
sl 3 sts onto cn, hold in back, k3, k3 from cn
sl 3 sts onto cn, hold in front, k3, k3 from cn
sl 4 sts onto cn, hold in back, k4, k4 from cn
sl 4 sts onto cn, hold in front, k4, k4 from cn
sl 5 sts onto cn, hold in back, k5, k5 from cn
sl 5 sts onto cn, hold in front, k5, k5 from cn
sl 6 sts onto cn, hold in back, k6, k6 from cn
sl 6 sts onto cn, hold in front, k6, k6 from cn
sl 7 sts onto cn, hold in front, k7, k7 from cn

DECREASE

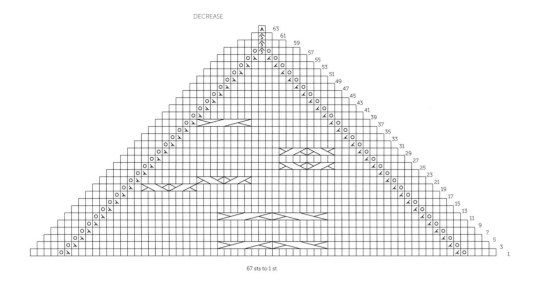

67 sts to 1 st

☐	knit
Ⓞ	yo
⬠	k3tog
⬠	sssk
⬠	sl 2 as if to k2tog, k1, p2sso
⬠	sl 3 as if to k3tog, k2tog, p3sso

sl 1 st onto cn, hold in back, k1, k1 from cn
sl 1 st onto cn, hold in front, k1, k1 from cn
sl 2 sts onto cn, hold in back, k2, k2 from cn
sl 2 sts onto cn, hold in front, k2, k2 from cn
sl 3 sts onto cn, hold in back, k3, k3 from cn
sl 3 sts onto cn, hold in front, k3, k3 from cn
sl 4 sts onto cn, hold in back, k4, k4 from cn
sl 4 sts onto cn, hold in front, k4, k4 from cn
sl 5 sts onto cn, hold in back, k5, k5 from cn
sl 5 sts onto cn, hold in front, k5, k5 from cn
sl 6 sts onto cn, hold in back, k6, k6 from cn
sl 6 sts onto cn, hold in front, k6, k6 from cn
sl 7 sts onto cn, hold in front, k7, k7 from cn

TRURO

PULLOVER

Amanda Scheuzger

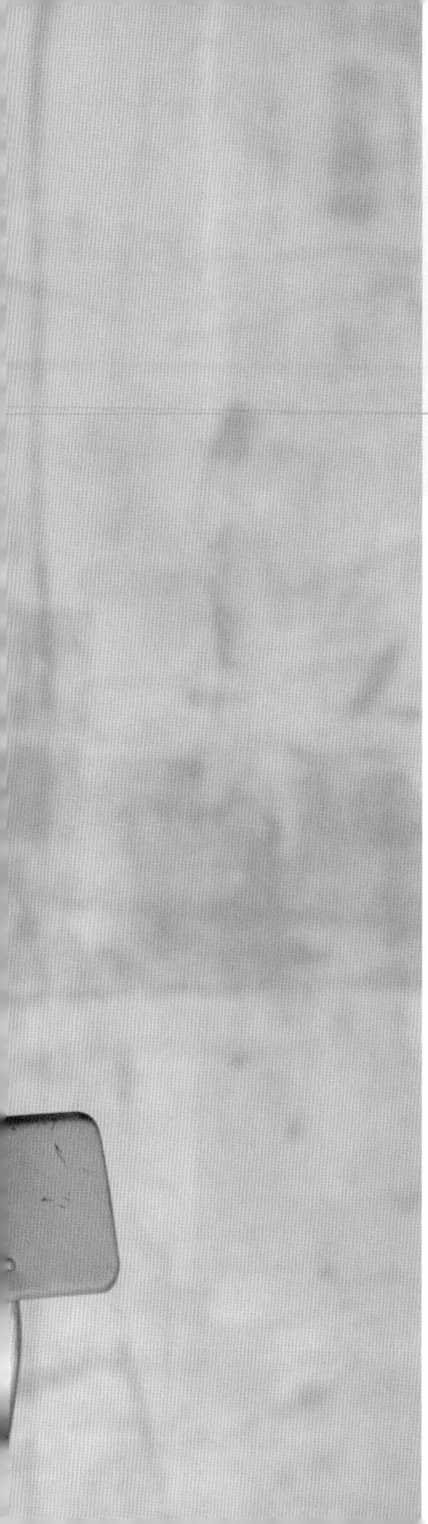

The Truro Pullover features garter rib and a fascinating raglan-sleeve construction. Worked from the bottom up in one piece, the pullover's cable-ribbed sleeves are joined to the body, and the unusual yoke is worked up to the collar.

FINISHED SIZE

35¼ (38¾, 42¾, 47¼, 51¼)" (89.5 [98.5, 108.5, 120, 130] cm) bust circumference. Pullover shown measures 38¾" (98.5 cm); modeled with 3¾" (9.5 cm) of positive ease.

YARN

DK weight (#3)

SHOWN HERE: Ancient Arts Fibre Crafts Superwash Merino DK (100% superwash merino; 220 yd [200 m]/3½ oz [100 g]): Russian (silver) blue, 7 (8, 9, 9, 10) skeins.

NEEDLES

Size U.S. 6 (4 mm): 16" and 32" circular (cir) and set of double-pointed (dpn).

Size U.S. 7 (4.5 mm): 16" and 32" cir and set of dpn.

Adjust needle size if necessary to obtain the correct gauge.

NOTIONS

Markers (m); stitch holders; cable needle (cn); tapestry needle.

GAUGE

24 sts and 32 rnds = 4" (10 cm) in garter rib patt on larger needle; 25½ sts and 32 rnds = 4" (10 cm) in cable patt on larger needle.

NOTES

- This sweater is worked in the round from the bottom up. The body and sleeves are worked to the underarm, inserting the pocket lining in the lower body, then the sleeves and body are joined to work the yoke with raglan decs. The decs are concentrated on the body to create an exaggerated raglan line. Additional decs are placed in the center of each sleeve to shape the shoulders.

- During shaping, if there are not enough sts to work a complete cable, work the sts in stockinette st instead.

STITCH GUIDE

GARTER RIB PATTERN:
(MULTIPLE OF 4 STS)

RND 1: Knit.

RND 2: *P1, k3; rep from * to end.

Rep Rnds 1 and 2 for patt.

DEC2RC

Sl 2 sts onto cn, hold in back, parallel to left needle, *insert right needle into first st on left needle then into first st on cn and k2tog; rep from * once more—2 sts dec'd.

DEC2LC

Sl 2 sts onto cn, hold in front, parallel to left needle, *insert right needle into first st on cn then into first st on left needle and k2tog; rep from * once more—2 sts dec'd.

DEC3RC

Sl 3 sts onto cn, hold in back, parallel to left needle, *insert right needle into first st on left needle then into first st on cn and k2tog; rep from * 2 more times—3 sts dec'd.

DEC3LC

Sl 3 sts onto cn, hold in front, parallel to left needle, *insert right needle into first st on cn then into first st on left needle and k2tog; rep from * 2 more times—3 sts dec'd.

INSTRUCTIONS

POCKET LINING

With smaller needle, CO 25 sts. Do not join.

NEXT ROW: (RS) P1, *k3, p1; rep from * to end.

NEXT ROW: (WS) Purl.

Rep last 2 rows until piece measures 3½" (9 cm) from CO, ending with a RS row. Place sts on holder. Break yarn and set aside.

BODY

With smaller 32" cir needle, CO 212 (232, 256, 284, 308) sts. Place marker (pm) and join in the rnd.

Work in Garter Rib patt (see Stitch Guide) until piece measures 4" (10 cm) from CO, ending with Rnd 2. Change to larger 32" cir needle.

PLACE POCKET

NEXT RND: K12 (16, 20, 24, 24), place next 25 sts on holder for pocket edging, k25 pocket lining sts from holder, knit to end.

Cont in patt until piece measures 16" (40.5 cm) from CO, ending with Rnd 2. Do not break yarn. Set aside.

RIGHT SLEEVE

With smaller dpn, CO 52 (52, 52, 60, 60) sts. Pm and join in the rnd. Work Right Sleeve chart until piece measures 1" (2.5 cm) from CO.

Change to larger dpn. Cont in patt until piece measures 2" (5 cm) from CO, ending with an odd-numbered chart rnd.

INC RND: Work 1 st in patt, M1L, work in patt to end, M1R—2 sts inc'd.

Rep inc rnd every 6th (6th, 4th, 4th, 2nd) rnd 8 (18, 16, 25, 10) more times, then every 8 (0, 6, 0, 4)th rnd 7 (0, 7, 0, 21) times, working new sts into patt, and

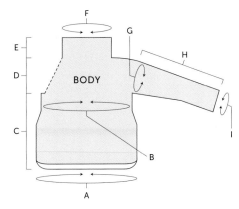

A: 41¼ (45¾, 50¼, 54¾, 59½, 64)"
(105 [116, 127.5, 141.5, 151, 162.5] cm)

B: 36½ (41¼, 45¾, 50¼, 54¾, 59½)"
(92.5 [105, 127.5, 141.5, 151] cm)

C: 15 (15, 15¼, 15¼, 15½, 15½)"
(38 [38, 38.5, 38.5, 39.5, 39.5] cm)

D: 7 (7½, 8, 8½, 9, 9½)"
(18 [19, 20.5, 21.5, 23, 24] cm)

E: 4" (10 cm)

F: 20¼ (21¾, 23¼, 26¼, 27¾, 29¼)"
(51.5 [55, 59, 66.5, 70.5, 64.5] cm)

G: 13¼ (14¾, 16¼, 17¾, 19¼, 20¾)"
(33.5 [37.5, 41.5, 45, 49, 52.5] cm)

H: 17½" (44.5 cm)

I: 8½ (9¼, 9¾, 10½, 10¾, 11½)"
(21.5 [23.5, 25, 26.5, 27.5, 29] cm)

changing to larger 16" cir needle when necessary—84 (90, 100, 112, 124) sts.

Work even until piece measures 18" (45.5 cm) from CO, ending with Rnd 3 or 7 of chart.

NEXT RND: Work in patt to last 8 (9, 10, 12, 14) sts, place next 17 (19, 21, 25, 29) sts on holder for underarm, removing m—67 (71, 79, 87, 95) sts rem. Place sts on separate holder.

LEFT SLEEVE

Work as for right sleeve, foll Left Sleeve chart.

YOKE

JOIN BODY AND SLEEVES

With larger 32" cir needle and yarn attached to body, work 9 (10, 11, 13, 15) body sts in patt, place last 17 (19, 21, 25, 29) body sts worked on holder for underarm, work 89 (97, 107, 117, 125) body sts in patt for front, place next 17 (19, 21, 25, 29) body sts on holder for underarm, pm, work 67 (71, 79, 87, 95) right sleeve sts in patt, pm, work 89 (97, 107, 117, 125) body sts in patt for back, pm, work 67 (71, 79, 87, 95) left sleeve sts in patt—312 (336, 372, 408, 440) sts.

Pm and join in the rnd. Work 1 rnd even in patt.

NEXT RND: *K1, k2tog, work in patt to 3 sts before m, ssk, k1, sl m, k2tog, work in patt to 2 sts before m, ssk, sl m; rep from * once more—8 sts dec'd. Work 1 rnd even in patt.

Sizes 42¾ (51¼)" (111 [130] cm) only

SLEEVE DEC RND: *Work in patt to m, sl m, Dec2RC (see Stitch Guide), work in patt to 4 sts before m, Dec2LC (see Stitch Guide), sl m; rep from * once more—8 sts dec'd.

Work 1 rnd even in patt.

All sizes

DEC RND: *K1, k2tog, work in patt to 3 sts before m, ssk, k1, sl m, Dec2RC (see Stitch Guide), work in patt to 4 sts before

m, Dec2LC (see Stitch Guide), sl m; rep from * once more—12 sts dec'd.

Rep dec rnd every other rnd 0 (1, 0, 1, 0) more time—292 (304, 344, 376, 412) sts rem: 61 (61, 69, 77, 85) sts each sleeve, 85 (91, 103, 111, 121) sts each for front and back.

Work 1 (3, 5, 5, 1) rnd(s) even in patt.

BODY DEC RND: *Dec3RC (see Stitch Guide), work in patt to 6 sts before m, Dec3LC (see Stitch Guide), sl m, work in patt to next m, sl m; rep from * once more—12 sts dec'd.

Rep body dec rnd every 4th rnd 6 (3, 5, 1, 4) more time(s)—208 (256, 272, 352, 352) sts rem: 61 (61, 69, 77, 85) sts each sleeve, 43 (67, 67, 99, 91) sts each for front and back.

Sizes 38¾ (47¼)" (98.5 [120] cm) only

Work 1 rnd even in patt.

DEC RND: *K2tog, work in patt to 2 sts before m, ssk, sl m, work in patt to m, sl m; rep from * once more—4 sts dec'd.

Work 1 rnd even in patt.

NEXT RND: Rep body dec rnd—12 sts dec'd. Rep last 4 rnds 2 (3) more times—208 (288) sts rem.

All sizes

Work 1 rnd even in patt.

SHAPE SHOULDER: Next rnd *K2tog, work in patt to 2 sts before m, ssk, sl m, work 26 (26, 30, 34, 38) sts in patt, ssk, pm (for shoulder shaping), work 5 center sleeve sts in patt, pm (for shoulder shaping), k2tog, work in patt to m, sl m; rep from * once more—8 sts dec'd.

Sizes 42¾ (47¼, 51¼)" (108.5 [120, 130] cm) only

Work 1 rnd even in patt.

DEC RND: *Dec3RC, work in patt to 6 sts before m, Dec3LC, sl m, work in patt to 2 sts before shoulder m, ssk, sl m, work 5 sts in patt, sl m, k2tog, work in patt to m, sl m; rep from * once more—16 sts dec'd.

Work 1 rnd even in patt.

DEC RND: *K2tog, [work in patt to 2 sts before m, ssk, sl m] 2 times, work 5 sts in patt, sl m, k2tog, work in patt to m, sl m; rep from * once more—8 sts dec'd.

Rep last 4 rnds 1 (1, 3) more time(s)—216 (232, 248) sts rem.

All sizes

200 (200, 216, 232, 248) sts rem: 59 (59, 59, 67, 67) sts for each sleeve, 41 (41, 49, 49, 57) sts each for front and back; yoke measures 4¼ (4¾, 5½, 5½, 5½)" (11 [12, 14, 14, 14] cm).

Shape neck using short-rows, as foll:

SHORT-ROW 1: (RS) Work 6 sts in patt, wrap next st, turn.

SHORT-ROW 2: (WS) Work to 8th m at right front raglan, sl m, work 6 sts in patt, wrap next st, turn.

SHORT-ROW 3: *Dec3LC, sl m, work in patt to 2 sts before m, ssk, sl m, work 5 sts in patt, sl m, k2tog, work in patt to m, sl m, Dec3RC*, work in patt to 6 sts before m, rep from * to * once more, work wrap tog with wrapped st, work 2 sts in patt, wrap next st, turn—16 sts dec'd.

SHORT-ROW 4: Work to wrapped st, work wrap tog with wrapped st, work 2 sts, wrap next st, turn.

SHORT-ROW 5: *[Work in patt to 2 sts before m, ssk, sl m] 2 times, work 5 sts in patt, sl m, k2tog, work in patt to m, sl m, k2tog; rep from * once more, work in patt to wrapped st, work wrap tog with wrapped st, work 2 sts, wrap next st, turn—8 sts dec'd.

SHORT-ROW 6: Rep Short-row 4.

SHORT-ROW 7: *Work in patt to 6 sts before m, Dec3LC, sl m, work in patt to 2 sts before m, ssk, sl m, work 5 sts in patt, sl m, k2tog, work in patt to m, sl m, Dec3RC; rep from * once more, work to wrapped st, work wrap tog with st, work 2 sts in patt, wrap next st, turn—16 sts dec'd.

SHORT-ROW 8: Rep Short-row 4.

NEXT RND: *[Work in patt to 2 sts before m, ssk, sl m] 2 times, work 5 sts in patt, sl m, k2tog, work in patt to m, sl m, k2tog; rep from * once more, work in patt to wrapped st, work wrap tog with wrapped st, work 2 sts—152 (152, 168, 184, 200) sts rem: 51 (51, 51, 59, 59) sts for each sleeve, 25 (25, 33, 33, 41) sts each for front and back.

Pm for new beg of rnd at left side of front neck. Work 1 rnd even in patt.

NOTE: *As you work the following shaping, change to larger 16" circular needle when necessary.*

RAGLAN DEC RND: *Work in patt to 6 sts before m, Dec3LC, sl m, work in patt to 2 sts before m, ssk, sl m, work 5 sts in patt, sl m, k2tog, work in patt to m, sl m, Dec3RC; rep from * once more, work to end—16 sts dec'd.

Work 1 rnd even in patt.

NEXT RND: *[Work in patt to 2 sts before m, ssk, sl m] 2 times, work 5 sts in patt, sl m, k2tog, work in patt to m, sl m, k2tog; rep from * once more, work to end—8 sts dec'd.

Work 1 rnd even in patt.

NEXT RND: Rep raglan dec rnd—112 (112, 128, 144, 160) sts rem: 45 (45, 45, 53, 53) sts for each sleeve, 11 (11, 19, 19, 27) sts each for front and back; yoke measures 6 (6½, 7¼, 7¼, 7¼)" (15 [16.5, 18.5, 18.5, 18.5] cm) at center back, and 1" less at center front.

NECKBAND

Work 4 rnds even in patt. Change to smaller 16" cir needle. Work even in patt until neckband measures 2½" (6.5 cm). BO all sts in patt.

FINISHING

Block to measurements. Graft under-arms using Kitchener st.

POCKET EDGING

Place 25 held pocket sts on smaller dpn, then with RS facing, CO 3 sts onto same needle so 3 new sts will be worked first.

APPLIED I-CORD

*K2, sl 1 kwise wyb, k1 pocket st, psso, do not turn, slide sts to other end of needle; rep from * until all pocket sts have been used—three I-cord sts rem.

Tack live sts at end of I-cord and CO sts from beg of I-cord to RS of body. Sew sides and bottom of pocket lining to WS of body. Weave in ends.

OJAI

TOP

Andrea Babb

With its undulating waves of abstract cables, fine-weight wool, and airy elegance, the Ojai Top is both a statement piece and a versatile layer for every season. This top is worked in one piece from side to side and divided for the neck opening. Two purl stitches highlight the shoulder line.

FINISHED SIZE

49½ (54, 56, 57½)" (125.5 [137, 142, 146] cm) bust circumference. Top shown measures 49½" (125.5 cm) on a model with a 34" (86.5 cm) bust.

YARN

Fingering (#1)

SHOWN HERE: Be Sweet Skinny Wool (100% merino wool; 180 yd [165 m]/⅞ oz [25 g]): #11b dark camel, 6 (7, 7, 8) balls.

NEEDLES

Size U.S. 8 (5 mm): 24" circular (cir) and two double-pointed (dpn).

Adjust needle size if necessary to obtain the correct gauge.

NOTIONS

Stitch holders; cable needle (cn); size E/4 (3.5 mm) crochet hook; tapestry needle.

GAUGE

22 sts and 34 rows = 4" (10 cm) in St st.

NOTES

- This top is worked in one piece from side to side and divided for the neck opening. Two purl sts highlight the shoulder line.

- A cir needle is used to accommodate the large number of sts.

- Sl st at beg of RS rows kwise with yarn in back; sl st at beg of WS rows pwise with yarn in front.

BACK

With smaller straight needles and using the long-tail method, CO 98 (106, 114, 122, 130) sts.

NEXT ROW: K1, *k1, p1; rep from * to last st, k1.

Rep last row until piece measures ¾" (2 cm) from CO, ending with a WS row.

Change to larger needles. Work in St st, keeping 1 st at each edge in garter st, until piece measures 14½ (15¼, 15¼, 15½, 15½)" (37 [38.5, 38.5, 39.5, 39.5] cm) from CO, ending with a WS row.

SHAPE ARMHOLES

Place removable m at each end of row to mark beg of armhole.

INC ROW: (RS) K3, RLI, knit to last 3 sts, LLI, k3—2 sts inc'd.

Rep inc row every 6th row 3 more times—106 (114, 122, 130, 138) sts.

Work even until armhole measures 6 (6½, 7, 7½, 8)" (15 [16.5, 18, 19, 20.5] cm), ending with a WS row.

Shape shoulders using German short-rows as foll:

SHORT-ROW 1: (RS) Work to last 4 (3, 5, 4, 5) sts, turn.

SHORT-ROW 2: (WS) Make double st, work to last 4 (3, 5, 4, 5) sts, turn.

SHORT-ROWS 3 AND 4: Make double st, work to 3 (3, 3, 3, 4) sts before double st, turn.

Rep last 2 short-rows 5 (6, 6, 7, 1) more time(s).

Size 52" (132 cm) only

SHORT-ROWS 5 AND 6: Make double st, work to 3 sts before double st, turn.

Rep last 2 short-rows 5 more times.

ALL SIZES

NEXT ROW: (RS) Make double st, work to end, working each double st as a single st.

NEXT ROW: (WS) Work 32 (35, 37, 40, 42) sts and place these sts on holder for left shoulder, BO 42 (44, 48, 50, 54) sts, work to end, working each double st as a single st—32 (35, 37, 40, 42) sts rem for right shoulder. Place sts on holder.

FRONT

Work as for back until armhole measures 3 (3¾, 3¾, 4½, 4½)" (7.5 [9.5, 9.5, 11.5, 11.5] cm), ending with a WS row—106 (114, 122, 130, 138) sts.

SHAPE NECK

NEXT ROW: (RS) K46 (49, 51, 54, 56) and place these sts on holder for left front, BO 14 (16, 20, 22, 26) sts, knit to end—46 (49, 51, 54, 56) sts rem for right front.

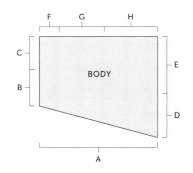

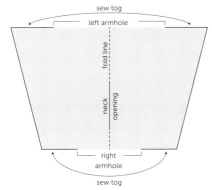

A: 24¾ (27, 28, 28¾)"
(63 [68.5, 71, 73] cm)

B: 7½ (8, 8½, 9)"
(19 [20.5, 21.5, 23] cm)

C: 6¾ (7¼, 7¾, 8½)"
(17 [18.5, 19.5, 21.5] cm)

D: 9 (9½, 10, 10½)"
(23 [24, 25.5, 26.5] cm)

E: 11¾ (12¼, 13, 13½)"
(30 [31.5, 33, 34.5] cm)

F: 4 (4¼, 4¼, 4¼)"
(10 [11, 11, 11] cm)

G: 9½ (10, 10, 10)"
(24 [25.5, 25.5, 25.5] cm)

H: 11¼ (12¾, 13¾, 14½)"
(28.5 [32, 35, 37] cm)

TOP

CO 228 (240, 252, 264) sts. Do not join.

NEXT ROW: (WS) Sl 1 (see Notes), p112 (118, 124, 130), k2, purl to end.

NEXT ROW: (RS) Sl 1, k112 (118, 124, 130), p2, knit to end.

Rep last 2 rows once more, then work WS row again.

NEXT ROW: (RS) Sl 1, k40 (46, 52, 58), [k12, place next 12 sts on holder] 3 times, p2, [place next 12 sts on holder, k12] 3 times, knit to end—156 (168, 180, 192) sts rem.

Work 19 (21, 21, 21) rows even, ending with a WS row.

WORK CABLES

Transfer 12 sts from one holder to dpn and, with RS facing, rejoin yarn. Work in St st for 20 (22, 22, 22) rows, ending with a WS row. Break yarn. Place sts on holder. Rep for all rem sts on holders.

Rejoin sts as foll:

NEXT ROW: (RS) With cir needle, sl 1, k40 (46, 52, 58), [k12 from holder, k12] 3 times, p2, [k12, k12 from holder] 3 times, knit to end—228 (240, 252, 264) sts.

Work 5 rows even, ending with a WS row.

NEXT ROW: (RS) Sl 1, k40 (46, 52, 58), [k12, place next 12 sts on holder] 3 times, p2, [place next 12 sts on holder, k12] 3 times, knit to end—156 (168, 180, 192) sts rem.

Work 3 rows even, ending with a WS row.

DIVIDE FOR NECK

NOTE: *Both sides of neck are worked simultaneously, each with its own ball of yarn; a semicolon between instructions separates the two sides.*

NEXT ROW: (RS) Sl 1, k76 (82, 88, 94), sl 1 purl st to cn, hold in front, p1; join new yarn, p1 from cn, knit to end—78 (84, 90, 96) sts each for front and back.

Working each side separately and sl st at each neck edge every other row, work 15 (17, 17, 17) rows even, ending with a WS row.

WORK CABLES

Transfer 12 sts from one holder to dpn and, with RS facing, rejoin yarn. Work in St st for 20 (22, 22, 22) rows, ending with a WS row. Break yarn. Place sts on holder. Rep for all rem sts on holders.

Rejoin sts as foll:

NEXT ROW: (RS) With cir needle, sl 1, k40 (46, 52, 58), [k12 from holder, k12] 3 times, p1; sl 1, [k12, k12 from holder] 3 times, knit to end—114 (120, 126, 132) sts each for front and back.

Work 5 rows even, ending with a WS row.

NEXT ROW: (RS) Sl 1, k64 (70, 76, 82), [k12, place next 12 sts on holder] 2 times, p1; sl 1, [place next 12 sts on holder, k12] 2 times, knit to end—90 (96, 102, 108) sts rem each for front and back.

Work 19 (21, 21, 21) rows even, ending with a WS row.

WORK CABLES

Transfer 12 sts from one holder to dpn and, with RS facing, rejoin yarn. Work in St st for 20 (22, 22, 22) rows, ending with a WS row. Break yarn. Place sts on holder. Rep for all rem sts on holders. Rejoin sts as foll:

NEXT ROW: (RS) With cir needle, sl 1, k64 (70, 76, 82), [k12 from holder, k12] 2 times, p1; sl 1, [k12, k12 from holder] 2 times, knit to end—114 (120, 126, 132) sts each for front and back.

Work 5 rows even, ending with a WS row.

NEXT ROW: (RS) Sl 1, k64 (70, 76, 82), [k12, place next 12 sts on holder] 2 times, p1; sl 1, [place next 12 sts on holder, k12] 2 times, knit to end—90 (96, 102, 108) sts rem each for front and back.

Work 19 (21, 21, 21) rows even, ending with a WS row.

WORK CABLES

Transfer 12 sts from one holder to dpn and, with RS facing, rejoin yarn. Work in St st for 20 (22, 22, 22) rows, ending with a WS row. Break yarn. Place sts on holder. Rep for all rem sts on holders.

Rejoin sts as foll:

NEXT ROW: (RS) With cir needle, sl 1, k64 (70, 76, 82), [k12 from holder, k12] 2 times, p1; sl 1, [k12, k12 from holder] 2 times, knit to end—114 (120, 126, 132) sts each for front and back.

Work 5 rows even, ending with a WS row.

NEXT ROW: (RS) Sl 1, k100 (106, 112, 118), place next 12 sts on holder, p1; sl 1, place next 12 sts on holder, knit to end—102 (108, 114, 120) sts rem each for front and back.

Work 5 rows even, ending with a WS row. Break 2nd ball of yarn.

JOIN FRONT AND BACK

NEXT ROW: (RS) Sl 1, knit to last st of front, sl 1 purl st to cn, hold in front, with same yarn, p1, p1 from cn, knit to end—204 (216, 228, 240) sts.

Work 13 (15, 15, 15) rows even, ending with a WS row.

WORK CABLES

Transfer 12 sts from one holder to dpn and, with RS facing, rejoin yarn. Work in St st for 20 (22, 22, 22) rows, ending with a WS row. Break yarn. Place sts on holder. Rep for rem sts on holder.

Rejoin sts as foll:

NEXT ROW: (RS) With cir needle, sl 1, k88 (94, 100, 106), k12 from holder, k12, p2, k12, k12 from holder, knit to end—228 (240, 252, 264) sts.

Work 5 rows even, ending with a WS row.

NEXT ROW: (RS) Sl 1, k100 (106, 112, 118), place next 12 sts on holder, p2, place next 12 sts on holder, knit to end—204 (216, 228, 240) sts rem.

Work 19 (21, 21, 21) rows even, ending with a WS row.

WORK CABLES

Transfer 12 sts from one holder to dpn and, with RS facing, rejoin yarn. Work in St st for 20 (22, 22, 22) rows, ending with a WS row. Break yarn. Place sts on holder. Rep for rem sts on holder. Rejoin sts as foll:

NEXT ROW: (RS) With cir needle, sl 1, k88 (94, 100, 106), k12 from holder, k12, p2, k12, k12 from holder, knit to end—228 (240, 252, 264) sts.

Work 55 (63, 71, 79) rows even, ending with a WS row. Loosely BO all sts.

FINISHING

Weave in ends. Block to measurements, being careful not to flatten cables.

RIGHT ARMHOLE EDGING

Fold and pin each cable end so center 6 sts are centered on selvedge. Beg at lower edge, sew right side seam for 7½ (8, 8½, 9)" (19 [20.5, 21.5, 23] cm).

With crochet hook and 2 strands of yarn held tog, work 1 rnd of single crochet around armhole, working through pinned cable folds. Beg at lower edge, sew left side seam for 9 (9½, 10, 10½)" (23 [24, 25.5, 26.5] cm).

NOTE: *Left armhole opening does not need a crocheted edging.*

HARTWICH

TOP

Norah Gaughan

Chic and comfortable, the Hartwich Top is worked from the bottom up and ends with traditional circular yoke construction, but with its twisted sleeve cuffs and cropped length, this top is anything but traditional. Featuring Woolfolk Får, a lofty and uber-soft merino chainette, this top is as light as a feather, soft to the touch, and deliciously warm—a true winter wardrobe staple.

FINISHED SIZE

34 (38, 42, 46, 50, 54)" (86.5 [96.5, 106.5, 117, 127, 137] cm) bust circumference. Pullover shown measures 38" (96.5 cm); modeled with 4" (10 cm) of positive ease.

YARN

Worsted weight (#4)

SHOWN HERE: Woolfolk Får (100% Ovis 21 ©Ultimate Merino; 142 yd [130 m]/ 1¾ oz [50 g]): #03 gray, 8 (8, 9, 10, 11, 12) skeins.

NEEDLES

Sizes U.S. 7 (4.5 mm): 24" circular (cir) and set of double-pointed (dpn).

Adjust needle size if necessary to obtain the correct gauge.

NOTIONS

Markers (m); removable m; stitch holders; tapestry needle.

GAUGE

20 sts and 28 rnds = 4" (10 cm) in St st.

NOTES

- The chainette structure of the yarn makes it very stretchy, and the final results are hard to predict. Measure gauge carefully after the swatch has been steamed or after it has been wet-blocked and allowed to dry overnight.

- The bottom bands for the body and twisted sleeve bands are worked back and forth from side to side. Sts for the body and sleeves are picked up along the bands and worked separately in the round to the underarm, then the sleeves and body are joined to work the yoke.

- In the schematic, the right sleeve is shown separately from the body in order to present its cuff twist and balloon shape more clearly.

STITCH GUIDE

HALF TWISTED RIB (EVEN NUMBER OF STS)

ROW 1: K1, *p1, k1tbl; rep from * to last st, k1.

Rep Row 1 for patt.

INSTRUCTIONS

BOTTOM BANDS (MAKE 2)

CO 12 sts. Work in Half Twisted Rib (see Stitch Guide) for 17 (19, 21, 23, 25, 27)" (43 [48.5, 54, 58.5, 63.5, 68.5] cm). BO all sts in patt.

BODY

With cir needle and RS facing, pick up and knit 85 (95, 105, 115, 125, 135) sts evenly along one long edge of one bottom band, place marker (pm) for side, then pick up and knit 85 (95, 105, 115, 125, 135) sts evenly along one long edge of 2nd bottom band—170 (190, 210, 230, 250, 270) sts. Pm and join in the rnd.

Work in St st until piece measures 9½ (10, 10½, 11, 11½, 12)" (24 [23.5, 26.5, 28, 29, 30.5] cm) from bottom edge of bands, ending 5 (6, 7, 8, 9, 10) sts before end of rnd on last rnd.

DIVIDE FOR FRONT AND BACK

NEXT RND: BO 10 (12, 14, 16, 18, 20) sts, removing m, knit to 5 (6, 7, 8, 9, 10) sts before side m, BO 10 (12, 14, 16, 18, 20) sts, removing m, knit to end—75 (83, 91, 99, 107, 115) sts each rem for front and back. Place sts on holders. Do not break yarn. Set aside.

SLEEVE BANDS (MAKE 2)

CO 26 sts. Work in Half Twisted Rib for 13 (14, 15, 16, 17, 18)" (33 [35.5, 38, 40.5, 43, 45.5] cm). BO all sts. Don't break yarn.

RIGHT SLEEVE

Place removable m in center of each long edge of band (red dots in **FIGURE 1**). Hold band horizontally with RS facing.

With dpn, pick up and knit 33 (35, 38, 40, 43, 45) sts along upper edge to m (green line in **FIGURE 1**), then fold lower edge up in front, bringing two m tog, and beg at lower edge m, pick up and knit 33 (35, 38, 40, 43, 45) sts along lower edge (**FIGURE 2**)—66 (70, 76, 80, 86, 90) sts. Pm and join in the rnd.

NEXT RND: [K11 (12, 13, 14, 15, 16), pm] 2 times, k22 (22, 24, 24, 26, 26) center sts, [pm, k11 (12, 13, 14, 15, 16)] 2 times.

INC RND: [Knit to m, M1R, sl m] 2 times, [knit to m, sl m, M1L] 2 times, knit to end—4 sts inc'd. Rep inc rnd every other rnd 3 more times—82 (86, 92, 96, 102, 106) sts.

Work even until piece measures 2" (5 cm) from pick-up rnd.

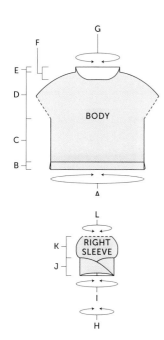

FIGURE 1    FIGURE 2

A: 34 (38, 42, 46, 50, 54)"
(86.5 [9.5, 106.5, 117, 127, 137] cm)

B: 1½" (3.8 cm)

C: 8 (8½, 9, 9½, 10, 10½)"
(20.5 [21.5, 23, 24, 25.5, 26.5] cm)

D: 8¾ (9¼, 9¾, 10¼, 10¾, 11¼)"
(22 [23.5, 25, 26, 27.5, 28.5] cm)

E: ¾" (2 cm)

F: 2¼" (5.5 cm)

G: 18¼ (20, 21¼, 23, 24¾, 26)"
(46.5 [51, 54, 58.5, 63, 66] cm)

H: 13¼ (14, 15¼, 16, 17¼, 18)"
(33.5 [35.5, 38.5, 40.5, 44, 45.5] cm)

I: 16½ (17¼, 18½, 19¼, 20½, 21¼)"
(42 [44, 47, 49, 52, 56.5] cm)

J: 3½" (9 cm)

K: 4½ (4½, 5, 5, 5½, 5½)"
(11.5 [11.5, 12.5, 12.5, 14, 14] cm)

L: 12½ (13¼, 14½, 15¼, 16½, 17¼)"
(31.5 [33.5, 37, 38.5, 42, 44] cm)

DEC RND: [Knit to 2 sts before m, ssk, sl m] 2 times, [knit to m, sl m, k2tog] 2 times, knit to end—4 sts dec'd.

Rep dec rnd every 4th rnd 4 more times—62 (66, 72, 76, 82, 86) sts rem.

Work even until piece measures 4½ (4½, 5, 5, 5½, 5½)" (11.5 [11.5, 12.5, 12.5, 14, 14] cm) from pick-up rnd, ending 5 (6, 7, 8, 9, 10) sts before end of rnd on last rnd.

NEXT RND: BO 10 (12, 14, 16, 18, 20) sts, removing m—52 (54, 58, 60, 64, 66) sts rem.

Place sts on holder. Break yarn.

LEFT SLEEVE

Work as for right sleeve, except bring lower edge of cuff band up in back so the twist will slant in the opposite direction. Do not place sts on holder.

YOKE

Place removable m in center front st and leave it there—37 (41, 45, 49, 53, 57) sts each side of marked st.

With cir needle and yarn still attached to body, k52 (54, 58, 60, 64, 66) left sleeve sts, k75 (83, 91, 99, 107, 115) front sts, k52 (54, 58, 60, 64, 66) right sleeve sts, k75 (83, 91, 99, 107, 115) back sts—254 (274, 298, 318, 342, 362) sts total.

Place removable m in 51st st on each side of center front m—103 sts total in marked section centered on front.

Work short-rows using the German method as foll:

SHORT-ROW 1: (RS) K38 (44, 52, 58, 66, 72) to first marked st, turn.

SHORT-ROW 2: (WS) Make double st, purl to marked st, turn—103 sts between turning points.

SHORT-ROW 3: Make double st, knit to double st, knit double st as a single st, k5, turn.

SHORT-ROW 4: Make double st, purl to double st, purl double st as a single st, p5, turn—10 fewer sts between turning points.

SHORT-ROWS 5–16: Rep Short-rows 3 and 4 six times—33 center front sts rem between turning points.

NEXT SHORT-ROW: Make double st, knit to end of rnd m, working double st as a single st. Knit 1 rnd, working last double st as a single st, removing m at each end of marked section, leaving center front m in place—yoke measures 2½" (6.5 cm) at center back and ¼" (6 mm) at center front.

Sizes 34 (42, 54)" (86.5 [106.5, 137] cm) only

Knit 1 rnd, dec 2 (4, 2) sts evenly across—252 (294, 360) sts rem.

Size 38" (96.5 cm) only

Knit 1 rnd, inc 2 sts evenly across—276 sts.

All sizes

Work even in St st until yoke measures 2¾ (3, 3¼, 3½, 3¾, 4)" (7 [7.5, 8.5, 9, 9.5, 10] cm) from m at center front.

DEC RND: [K4, k2tog] 42 (46, 49, 53, 57, 60) times—210 (230, 245, 265, 285, 300) sts rem.

Work even for 1½ (1¾, 2, 2¼, 2½, 2¾)" (3.8 [4.5, 5, 5.5, 6.5, 7] cm).

DEC RND: [K3, k2tog] 42 (46, 49, 53, 57, 60) times—168 (184, 196, 212, 228, 240) sts rem.

Work even for 1" (2.5 cm).

DEC RND: [K2, k2tog] 42 (46, 49, 53, 57, 60) times—126 (138, 147, 159, 171, 180) sts rem.

Work even for ¾" (2 cm).

DEC RND: [K1, k2tog] 42 (46, 49, 53, 57, 60) times—84 (92, 98, 106, 114, 120) sts rem; yoke measures about 6½ (7, 7½, 8, 8½, 9)" (16.5 [18, 19, 20.5, 21.5, 23] cm) from m at center front, and 8¾ (9¼, 9¾, 10¼, 10¾, 11¼)" (22 [23.5, 25, 26, 27.5, 28.5] cm) at center back.

Do not break yarn.

NECKBAND

CO 7 sts onto left needle.

ROWS 1, 3, AND 5: (RS) K1, [k1tbl, p1] 2 times, k1tbl, p2tog (1 band st and 1 body st), turn.

ROW 2 AND ALL WS ROWS: Sl 1 pwise wyf, [p1, k1tbl] 2 times, p1, k1.

ROW 7: K1, [k1tbl, p1] 2 times, k1tbl, p3tog (1 band st and 2 body sts), turn.

ROW 8: Rep Row 2.

Rep Rows 1–8 until no body sts rem. Graft live sts at end of band to band CO edge using Kitchener st.

FINISHING

Sew cuff seams. Sew underarms and weave in ends. Lightly steam block if necessary.

BIG SUR

PULLOVER

Norah Gaughan

Leave it to Norah Gaughan to take brioche stitch to the next level with an allover interrupted brioche texture in the Big Sur Pullover. The silhouette is oversized and features modern neckband details that are joined by grafting in the back.

FINISHED SIZE

43½ (48½, 51½, 56½, 59½, 64½)" (110.5 [123, 131, 143.5, 151, 164] cm) bust circumference. Pullover shown measures 48½" (123 cm); modeled with 14½" (37 cm) of positive ease.

YARN

Sportweight (#2)

SHOWN HERE: Imperial Yarn Denali (50% American alpaca, 50% American merino; 195 yd [178 m]/2 oz [56 g]): pearl gray, 8 (9, 10, 11, 12, 14) skeins.

NEEDLES

Size U.S. 2 (2.75 mm).

Size U.S. 3 (3.25 mm).

Adjust needle size if necessary to obtain the correct gauge.

NOTIONS

Removable marker (m); stitch holders; tapestry needle.

GAUGE

20 sts and 46 rows = 4" (10 cm) in Interrupted Brioche st on larger needles.

NOTES

- This pullover is worked from the bottom up in pieces and seamed.
- When working decs, count a st and its corresponding yo as one st.

STITCH GUIDE

ALTERNATE CABLE CO (ODD NUMBER OF STS)

Make a slipknot on needle, then using the long-tail method, CO another st onto same needle—2 sts. CO rem sts as foll: *Wyb, insert right needle from front to back between first 2 sts on left needle, wrap yarn as if to knit and draw yarn through, sl st kwise to left needle (1 knit st CO). Wyf, insert right needle from back to front between first 2 sts on left needle, wrap yarn as if to purl and draw yarn through, sl st kwise to left needle (1 purl st CO). Rep from *, ending with a knit st.

TUBULAR CO (ODD NUMBER OF STS)

Using the alternate cable method (see Stitch Guide), CO an odd number of sts.

NEXT ROW: (RS) *K1, sl 1 pwise wyf; rep from * to last st, k1.

NEXT ROW: (WS) *Sl 1 pwise wyf, k1; rep from * to last st, sl 1 pwise wyf.

YFSL1YO

Yarn forward between needles, sl next st pwise wyf, bring yarn over needle to back.

BRK

Knit st tog with its companion yo.

KNIT 1 BELOW (K1B)

Insert right needle from front to back into center of st below next st on left needle, wrap yarn and pull new st through—1 st inc'd.

INTERRUPTED BRIOCHE STITCH (ODD NUMBER OF STS)

ROW 1: (RS) K1, *yfsl1yo (see Stitch Guide), k1; rep from * to end.

ROW 2: (WS) K1, *brk (see Stitch Guide), yfsl1yo; rep from * to last 2 sts, brk, k1.

ROW 3: K1, *yfsl1yo, brk; rep from * to last 2 sts, yfsl1yo, k1.

ROW 4: Rep Row 2.

ROW 5: K1, *k1, brk; rep from * to last 2 sts, k2.

ROW 6: Purl.

Rep Rows 1–6 for patt.

INSTRUCTIONS

BACK

With smaller needles and using the tubular method (see Stitch Guide), CO 145 (161, 171, 187, 197, 213) sts. Work in k1, p1 rib until piece measures 1½" (3.8 cm) from CO, ending with a WS row. Change to larger needles.

NEXT ROW: (RS) K0 (0, 0, 0, 2, 2), [k2, k2tog] 36 (40, 42, 46, 48, 52) times, k1 (1, 3, 3, 3, 3)—109 (121, 129, 141, 149, 161) sts rem.

NEXT ROW: (WS) Purl.

Work in Interrupted Brioche st (see Stitch Guide) until piece measures 22 (23, 24, 25, 26, 27)" (56 [58.5, 61, 63.5, 66, 68.5] cm) from CO, ending with a WS row.

SHAPE SHOULDERS AND NECK

BO 3 (2, 3, 4, 3, 4) sts at beg of next 4 (8, 14, 4, 12, 14) rows, then BO 2 (3, 0, 3, 4, 0) sts at beg of next 10 (6, 0, 10, 2, 0) rows—77 (87, 87, 95, 105, 105) sts rem.

NEXT ROW: (RS) BO 2 (3, 3, 3, 4, 4) sts, work in patt until there are 24 (28, 28, 28, 32, 32) sts on right needle after BO, join a 2nd ball of yarn and BO center 25 (25, 25, 33, 33, 33) sts, work to end—24 (28, 28, 28, 32, 32) sts rem for right shoulder; 26 (31, 31, 31, 36, 36) sts rem for left shoulder.

NEXT ROW: For first group of sts, BO 2 (3, 3, 3, 4, 4) sts at armhole edge, work to center gap; for 2nd group of sts, BO 4 sts at neck edge, work to end.

Rep last row 7 more times—no sts rem for right shoulder; 2 (3, 3, 3, 4, 4) sts rem for left shoulder.

NEXT ROW: (WS) BO left shoulder sts—no sts rem.

FRONT

Work as back until piece measures 10 (11, 12, 12, 13, 14)" (25.5 [28, 30.5, 30.5, 33, 35.5] cm) from CO, ending with Row 4 of patt—109 (121, 129, 141, 149, 161) sts.

DIVIDE FOR V-NECK

NEXT ROW: (RS) Work 54 (60, 64, 70, 74, 80) sts in patt, join 2nd ball of yarn and BO 1 st, work in patt to end—54 (60, 64, 70, 74, 80) sts rem each side.

NEXT ROW: (WS) Working both sides at the same time, each with its own ball of yarn, purl.

ROWS 1–6: Work Rows 1–6 of patt.

ROWS 7–10: Work Rows 1–4 of patt.

ROW 11: (Row 5 of patt; RS dec row) Work in patt to 10 sts before neck edge, sssk, work 7 sts in patt; on right front, work 7 sts in patt, k3tog, work in patt to end—2 sts dec'd at each neck edge.

ROW 12: (Row 6 of patt; WS) Purl.

ROWS 13–18: Rep Rows 7–12—2 sts dec'd at each neck edge.

Rep last 18 rows 6 (6, 6, 7, 7, 7) more times—26 (32, 36, 38, 42, 48) sts rem each side.

Work even until piece measures 22 (23, 24, 25, 26, 27)" (56 [58.5, 61, 63.5, 66, 68.5] cm) from CO, ending with a WS row.

SHAPE SHOULDERS

BO 3 (2, 3, 4, 3, 4) sts at beg of next 4 (8, 24, 4, 12, 24) rows, then BO 2 (3, 0, 3, 4, 0) sts at beg of next 20 (16, 0, 20, 12, 0) rows—no sts rem.

SLEEVES

With smaller needles and using the tubular method, CO 69 (73, 77, 77, 81, 85) sts.

Work in k1, p1 rib until piece measures 1½" (3.8 cm) from CO, ending with a WS row. Change to larger needles.

Knit 1 row.

Purl 1 row.

Work in Interrupted Brioche st until piece measures 15" (38 cm) from CO, ending with Row 4 of patt.

SHAPE CAP

Sizes 43½ (51½ , 56½ , 64½)" (110.5 [131, 143.5, 164] cm) only

DEC ROW: (Row 5 of patt; RS) Work 2 sts, k3tog, work to last 5 sts, sssk, work 2 sts—65 (73, 73, 81) sts rem.

Work 5 rows even, ending with Row 4 of patt.

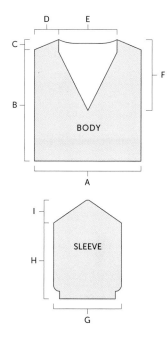

A: 21¾ (24¼, 25¾, 28¼, 29¾, 32¼)" (55 [61.5, 65.5, 72, 75.5, 82] cm)

B: 22 (23, 24, 25, 26, 27)" (56 [58.5, 61,63.5, 66, 68.5] cm)

C: 2" (5 cm)

D: 5¼ (6½, 7¼, 7½, 8½, 9½)" (13.5 [16.5, 18.5, 19, 21.5, 24] cm)

E: 11½ (11½, 11½, 13, 13, 13)" (29 [29, 29, 33, 33, 33] cm)

F: 14 (14, 14, 15, 15, 15)" (35.5 [35.5, 35.5, 38, 38, 38] cm)

G: 13¾ (14½, 15½, 15½, 16¼, 17)" (35 [37, 39.5, 39.5, 41.5, 43] cm)

H: 15" (38 cm)

I: 4½ (4½, 5¼, 5¼, 5¼, 5¾)" (11.5 [11.5, 13.5, 13.5, 13.5, 14.5] cm)

All sizes

DEC ROW: (Row 5 of patt; RS) Work 1 st, [work 1 st, k3tog] 2 times, work to last 9 sts, [sssk, work 1 st] 2 times, work 1 st—8 sts dec'd.

Rep dec row every 6th row 5 (6, 6, 6, 7, 7) more times—17 sts rem.

Work 5 rows even, ending with Row 4 of patt.

SHAPE POINT

NEXT ROW: (RS) K2, k3tog (first and 3rd sts are brk), k1, ssk (first st is a brk), brk, k2tog (2nd st is a brk), k1, sssk (first and 3rd sts are brk), k2—11 sts rem.

NEXT ROW: P4, sl 3 pwise wyf, p4.

NEXT ROW: [K1, yfsl1yo] 2 times, sl 2 as if to k2tog, k1, p2sso, [yfsl1yo, k1] 2 times—9 sts rem.

Work Rows 2–4 of patt.

NEXT ROW: K2, ssk (first st is a brk), brk, k2tog (2nd st is a brk), k2—7 sts rem.

NEXT ROW: P2, sl 3 pwise wyf, p2. Next row K2, sl 2 as if to k2tog, k1, p2sso, k2—5 sts rem.

NEXT ROW: K1, sl 3 pwise wyf, k1. Next row K1, sl 2 as if to k2tog, k1, p2sso, k1—3 sts rem. BO all sts.

NECKBAND

With smaller needles, CO 5 sts.

ROWS 1 AND 3: (WS) Purl.

ROW 2: (RS) Knit.

ROW 4: K2, yo, k1, yo, k2—7 sts.

ROWS 5 AND 7: P2, k1, p1, k1, p2.

ROW 6: K2, p1, k1, p1, k2.

ROW 8: K2, [yo, p1, yo, k1] 2 times, k1—11 sts.

ROWS 9 AND 11: [P3, k1] 2 times, p3.

ROW 10: [K3, p1] 2 times, k3.

ROW 12: K2, yo, k1, p1, k1, [yo, k1] 2 times, p1, k1, yo, k2—15 sts.

ROWS 13 AND 15: P2, [k1, p1] 6 times, p1.

ROW 14: K2, [p1, k1] 6 times, k1. Mark center st with removable m; move this m up as you work.

ROW 16: K2, yo, *p1, k1; rep from * to 1 st before center st, p1, yo, k1, yo, p1, **k1, p1; rep from ** to last 2 sts, yo, k2—4 sts inc'd.

ROWS 17 AND 19: P3, *k1, p1; rep from * to center st, p1, **p1, k1; rep from ** to last 3 sts, p3.

ROW 18: K3, *p1, k1; rep from * to center st, k1, **k1, p1; rep from ** to last 3 sts, k3.

ROW 20: K2, yo, *k1, p1; rep from * to 1 st before center st, [k1, yo] 2 times, **k1, p1; rep from ** to last 3 sts, k1, yo, k2—4 sts inc'd.

ROWS 21 AND 23: P2, *k1, p1; rep from * to last st, p1.

ROW 22: K2, *p1, k1; rep from * to last st, k1. Rep Rows 16–23 two more times—39 sts.

Work Rows 16–19 once—43 sts.

DIVIDE INTO 4 SECTIONS

NEXT ROW: (RS) K2, yo, [k1, p1] 3 times, k1, k1B (see Stitch Guide), place rem 34 sts on holder—11 sts on needle.

LEFT NECK SECTION

ROWS 1, 3, 5, AND 7: (WS) Sl 2 pwise wyf, *k1, p1; rep from * to last st, p1.

ROWS 2, 4, AND 6: K2, *p1, k1; rep from * to last st, k1.

ROW 8: K2, yo, *p1, k1; rep from * to last st, k1—1 st inc'd.

ROWS 9, 11, 13, AND 15: Sl 2 pwise wyf, *k1, p1; rep from * to last 2 sts, p2.

ROWS 10, 12, AND 14: K3, *p1, k1; rep from * to last st, k1.

ROW 16: K2, yo, *k1, p1; rep from * to last 2 sts, k2—1 st inc'd.

Rep Rows 1–16 three more times—19 sts.

NEXT ROW: (WS) Sl 2 pwise wyf, *k1, p1; rep from * to last st, p1.

NEXT ROW: (RS) K2, *p1, k1; rep from * to last st, k1.

Rep last 2 rows until band measures 4½ (4½ , 4½ , 5½, 5½ , 5½)" (11.5 [11.5, 11.5, 14, 14, 14] cm) from last yo.

Place sts on holder. Break yarn.

LEFT CENTER SECTION

With RS facing, return next 12 sts from holder to needle and rejoin yarn—22 sts rem on holder.

ROW 1: (RS) Sl 2 pwise wyb, [p1, k1] 5 times, k1B—13 sts.

ROW 2: (WS) Sl 2 pwise wyf, *k1, p1; rep from * to last st, p1.

ROW 3: (RS) Sl 2 pwise wyb, *p1, k1; rep from * to last st, k1.

ROWS 4–22: Rep Rows 2 and 3 nine times, then work Row 2 once more.

ROW 23: Sl 2 pwise wyb, p1, k3tog, *p1, k1; rep from * to last st, k1—2 sts dec'd.

ROWS 24–45: Rep Rows 2–23—9 sts rem.

Rep Rows 2 and 3 until piece measures 4½ (4½ , 4½, 5½ , 5½ , 5½)" (11.5 [11.5, 11.5, 14, 14, 14] cm) from last k3tog, ending with a RS row.

JOIN LEFT NECK AND LEFT CENTER SECTIONS

NEXT ROW: (WS) Sl 2 pwise wyf, [k1, p1] 3 times, sl last st of left center section to holder with left neck section sts, p2tog (last st of left center with first st of left neck), [p1, k1] 8 times, p2—27 sts.

ROW 1: (RS) Sl 2 pwise wyb, [p1, k1] 7 times, p1, k3tog, [p1, k1] 3 times, k1—25 sts rem.

ROWS 2, 4, 6, AND 8: (WS) Sl 2 pwise wyf, *k1, p1; rep from * to last st, p1.

ROWS 3, 5, AND 7: Sl 2 pwise wyb, *p1, k1; rep from * to last st, k1.

ROW 9: Sl 2 pwise wyb, [p1, k1] 6 times, p1, k3tog, [p1, k1] 3 times, k1—23 sts rem.

ROWS 10, 12, 14, AND 16: Sl 2 pwise wyf, *k1, p1; rep from * to last st, p1.

ROWS 11, 13, AND 15: Sl 2 pwise wyb, *p1, k1; rep from * to last st, k1.

ROW 17: Sl 2 pwise wyb, [p1, k1] 5 times, p1, k3tog, [p1, k1] 3 times, k1—21 sts rem.

ROW 18: Sl 2 pwise wyf, *k1, p1; rep from * to last st, p1.

ROW 19: Sl 2 pwise wyb, *p1, k1; rep from * to last st, k1.

Rep last 2 rows until piece measures 1 (1, 1, 1¾, 1¾, 1¾)" (2.5 [2.5, 2.5, 4.5, 4.5,

4.5] cm) from last k3tog, ending with a WS row. Break yarn, leaving a 12" (30.5 cm) tail. Place sts on holder.

RIGHT CENTER SECTION

Return next 12 sts to needle and, with RS facing, rejoin yarn—10 sts rem on holder.

ROW 1: (RS) Sl 2 pwise wyb, [p1, k1] 5 times, k1B—13 sts.

ROW 2: (WS) Sl 2 pwise wyf, *k1, p1; rep from * to last st, p1.

ROW 3: Sl 2 pwise wyb, *p1, k1; rep from * to last st, k1.

ROWS 4–22: Rep Rows 2 and 3 nine times, then work Row 2 once more.

ROW 23: Sl 2 pwise wyb, p1, *k1, p1; rep from * to last 6 sts, sssk, p1, k2—2 sts dec'd.

ROWS 24–45: Rep Rows 2–23—9 sts rem.

Rep Rows 2 and 3 until piece measures 4½ (4½, 4½, 5½, 5½, 5½)" (11.5 [11.5, 11.5, 14, 14, 14] cm) from last sssk, ending with a RS row. Break yarn. Place sts on holder.

RIGHT NECK SECTION

Return rem 10 sts to needle and, with RS facing, rejoin yarn.

ROW 1: (RS) Sl 2 pwise wyb, [p1, k1] 3 times, yo, k2—11 sts.

ROWS 2, 4, 6, AND 8: (WS) P2, *k1, p1; rep from * to last st, p1.

ROWS 3, 5, AND 7: Sl 2 pwise wyb, *p1, k1; rep from * to last st, k1.

ROW 9: Sl 2 pwise wyb, *p1, k1; rep from * to last 3 sts, p1, yo, k2—1 st inc'd.

ROWS 10, 12, 14, AND 16: P3, *k1, p1; rep from * to last st, p1.

ROWS 11, 13, AND 15: Sl 2 pwise wyb, *p1, k1; rep from * to last 2 sts, k2.

ROW 17: Sl 2 pwise wyb, *p1, k1; rep from * to last 2 sts, yo, k2—1 st inc'd.

Rep Rows 2–17 three more times—19 sts.

NEXT ROW: (WS) P2, *k1, p1; rep from * to last st, p1.

NEXT ROW: (RS) Sl 2 pwise wyb, *p1, k1; rep from * to last st, k1. Rep last 2 rows until band measures 4½ (4½, 4½, 5½, 5½, 5½)" (11.5 [11.5, 11.5, 14, 14, 14] cm) from last yo, ending with a RS row.

JOIN RIGHT NECK AND RIGHT CENTER SECTIONS

NEXT ROW: (WS) P2, [k1, p1] 8 times, sl last st of right neck section to holder with right center section sts, ssp (last st of right neck with first st of right center), [p1, k1] 3 times, p2—27 sts.

ROW 1: (RS) Sl 2 pwise wyb, [p1, k1] 2 times, p1, sssk, [p1, k1] 8 times, k1—25 sts rem.

ROWS 2, 4, 6, AND 8: P2, *k1, p1; rep from * to last st, p1.

ROWS 3, 5, AND 7: Sl 2 pwise wyb, *p1, k1; rep from * to last st, k1.

ROW 9: Sl 2 pwise wyb, [p1, k1] 2 times, p1, sssk, [p1, k1] 7 times, k1—23 sts rem.

ROWS 10, 12, 14, AND 16: P2, *k1, p1; rep from * to last st, p1.

ROWS 11, 13, AND 15: Sl 2 pwise wyb, *p1, k1; rep from * to last st, k1.

ROW 17: Sl 2 pwise wyb, [p1, k1] 2 times, p1, sssk, [p1, k1] 6 times, k1—21 sts rem.

ROW 18: P2, *k1, p1; rep from * to last st, p1.

ROW 19: Sl 2 pwise wyb, *p1, k1; rep from * to last st, k1.

Rep last 2 rows until piece measures 1 (1, 1, 1¾, 1¾, 1¾)" (2.5 [2.5, 2.5, 4.5, 4.5, 4.5] cm) from last sssk, ending with a WS row. Break yarn, leaving a 12" (30.5 cm) tail. Place sts on holder.

FINISHING

Block pieces to measurements. Sew shoulder seams.

Sew neckband into neck opening, stretching to fit; if necessary, return held sts to needles and add or remove rows so live sts meet at center back neck.

With RS facing, place knit sts of left neckband on one needle, then place purl sts from left neckband on another needle. Do the same for the sts of the right neckband.

With RS facing, use Kitchener st to graft the knit sts from right and left sides of neckband tog. Turn neckband so its WS is facing.

With knit side of rem live purl sts facing, use Kitchener st to graft right and left sides of neckband tog on WS.

Align center of each sleeve cap with shoulder seam, and working down from cap center, sew sides of cap smoothly to sides of body, making sure that armhole depth is the same on both front and back.

Sew sleeve and side seams. Weave in ends.

PROVINCETOWN

PULLOVER

Amanda Bell

The Provincetown Pullover is perfect for weekend escapes. This comfortably oversized cowl-neck pullover features large expanses of stockinette and reverse stockinette stitch for breezy knitting. Brioche stitch on the center front and cowl make this classic knit visually compelling and rewarding to the end.

FINISHED SIZE

39½ (43½, 47½, 51½, 55½)" (100.5 [110.5, 120.5, 131.5, 141] cm) bust circumference. Pullover shown measures 43½" (110.5 cm); modeled with 8½" (21.5 cm) of positive ease.

YARN

DK weight (#3)

SHOWN HERE: Sugar Bush Crisp (100% extrafine superwash merino; 95 yd [87 m]/1¾ oz [50 g]): #2018 titanium, 16 (17, 19, 20, 21) balls.

NEEDLES

Size U.S. 5 (3.75 mm): 24" circular (cir) and set of double-pointed (dpn).

Size U.S. 6 (4 mm): 24" cir.

Size U.S. 7 (4.5 mm): 24" cir and set of dpn.

Adjust needle size if necessary to obtain the correct gauge.

NOTIONS

Markers (m); stitch holders; tapestry needle.

GAUGE

20 sts and 29 rnds = 4" (10 cm) in St st on largest needle.

NOTES

• The body of this pullover is worked in the round from the lower edge to the underarm, then the front and back are worked separately back and forth. After the shoulders and underarms are seamed, sleeve sts are picked up, and the sleeves are worked in the round from the top down in reverse stockinette st by knitting on the WS.

• When binding off sts for front neckline, bind off normally to last st before brioche st panel, then lift last st to be dec up and over the last rem st on the right needle to avoid disrupting the brioche st.

BRIOCHE KNIT (BRK): Knit st tog with its companion yo.

SL1YO: Sl next st pwise wyf, bring yarn over needle to back.

BRIOCHE STITCH (ODD NUMBER OF STS)

ROW 1: (RS) Sl1yo (see Stitch Guide), *k1, sl1yo; rep from * to end.

ROW 2: (WS) Brk (see Stitch Guide), *sl1yo, brk; rep from * to end.

ROW 3: Sl1yo, *brk, sl1yo; rep from * to end.

Rep Rows 2 and 3 for patt.

BODY

With smallest cir needle, CO 186 (206, 226, 246, 266) sts. Place marker (pm) and join in the rnd.

Knit every st tbl for 6 rnds. Change to largest cir needle.

NEXT RND: P91 (101, 111, 121, 131) for front, pm for side, p95 (105, 115, 125, 135) for back.

NEXT RND: P1tbl, knit to 1 st before m, p1tbl, sl m, knit to end.

Rep last rnd until piece measures 5¾" from bottom of rolled edge.

INC RND: P1tbl, k1, M1L, k21 (24, 26, 29, 31), M1R, knit to 23 (26, 28, 31, 33) sts before m, M1L, knit to 2 sts before m, M1R, k1, p1tbl, sl m, k22 (25, 27, 30, 32), M1R, knit to 22 (25, 27, 30, 32) sts before m, M1L, knit to end—192 (212, 232, 252, 272) sts: 95 (105, 115, 125, 135) front sts, 97 (107, 117, 127, 137) back sts.

Working new sts in St st, work even until piece measures 11¼" (28.5 cm) from bottom of rolled edge.

INC RND: P1tbl, k1, M1L, k23 (26, 28, 31, 33), M1R, knit to 25 (28, 30, 33, 35) sts before m, M1L, knit to 2 sts before m, M1R, k1, p1tbl, sl m, k23 (26, 28, 31, 33), M1R, knit to 23 (26, 28, 31, 33) sts before m, M1L, knit to end—198 (218, 238, 258, 278) sts: 99 (109, 119, 129, 139) sts each for front and back.

Work even until piece measures 17¼ (17¼, 17¼, 16, 16)" (44 [44, 44, 40.5, 40.5] cm) from CO. Divide for front and back: Place first 99 (109, 119, 129, 139) sts on hold for front, removing m—99 (109, 119, 129, 139) sts rem for back.

BACK

SHAPE ARMHOLES

NEXT ROW: (WS) Using the backward-loop method, CO 6 sts, purl to end—105 (115, 125, 135, 145) sts.

NEXT ROW: (RS) CO 6 sts, knit to end—111 (121, 131, 141, 151) sts.

Work even until armhole measures 5¾ (6¼, 6¾, 7½, 8¼)" (14.5 [16, 17, 19, 21] cm), ending with a WS row.

SHAPE NECK

NEXT ROW: (RS) K34 (39, 42, 47, 52) and place these sts on holder for right shoulder, BO 43 (43, 47, 47, 47) sts, knit to end—34 (39, 42, 47, 52) sts rem for left shoulder.

LEFT SHOULDER

Purl 1 WS row—armhole measures 6 (6½, 7, 7¾, 8½)" (15 [16.5, 18, 19.5, 21.5] cm). Work neck decs while shaping shoulder using short-rows as foll:

SHORT-ROW 1: (RS) K1, ssk, knit to last 6 (7, 7, 8, 9) sts, wrap next st, turn—33 (38, 41, 46, 51) sts rem.

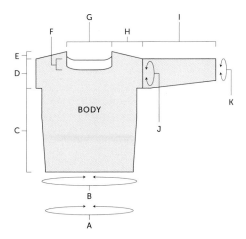

A: 37¼ (41¼, 45¼, 49¼, 53¼)"
(94.5 [105, 115, 125, 135] cm)

B: 39½ (43½, 47½, 51½, 55½)"
(1005 [110.5, 120.5, 131, 141] cm)

C: 17¼ (17¼, 17¼, 16, 16)"
(44 [44, 44, 40.5, 40.5] cm)

D: 6 (6½, 7, 7¾, 8½)"
(15 [16.5, 18, 19.5, 21.5] cm)

E: 1½" (3.8 cm)

F: 1¼" (3.2 cm)

G: 9½ (9½, 10¼, 10¼, 10¼)"
(24 [24, 26, 26, 26] cm)

H: 6½ (7½, 8, 9, 10)"
(16.5 [19, 20.5, 23, 25.5] cm)

I: 15½ (16, 16, 16½, 16½)"
(39.5 [40.5, 40.5, 42, 42] cm)

J: 12½ (13½, 14½, 16, 17½)"
(31.5 [34.5, 37, 40.5, 44.5] cm)

K: 9¼ (9¼, 9¼, 10, 10)"
(23.5 [23.5, 23.5, 25.5, 25.5] cm)

SHORT-ROWS 2, 4, 6, AND 8: (WS) Purl to end.

SHORT-ROW 3: K1, ssk, knit to 6 (6, 7, 8, 9) sts before wrapped st, wrap next st, turn—32 (37, 40, 45, 50) sts rem.

SHORT-ROW 5: Knit to 5 (6, 7, 8, 8) sts before wrapped st, wrap next st, turn.

SHORT-ROW 7: Knit to 5 (6, 7, 7, 8) sts before wrapped st, wrap next st, turn.

SHORT-ROW 9: Knit to 5 (6, 6, 7, 8) sts before wrapped st, wrap next st, turn.

SHORT-ROW 10: Purl to end.

BO all sts kwise, working wraps tog with wrapped sts as you come to them.

RIGHT SHOULDER

Return 34 (39, 42, 47, 52) held sts to needle and, with WS facing, rejoin yarn.

Purl 1 WS row.

NEXT ROW: (RS) Knit to last 3 sts, k2tog, k1—33 (38, 41, 46, 51) sts rem; armhole measures 6 (6½, 7, 7¾, 8½)" (15 [16.5, 18, 19.5, 21.5] cm). Complete neck decs while shaping shoulder using short-rows as foll:

SHORT-ROW 1: (WS) Purl to last 6 (7, 7, 8, 9) sts, wrap next st, turn.

SHORT-ROW 2: (RS) Knit to last 3 sts, k2tog, k1—32 (37, 40, 45, 50) sts rem.

SHORT-ROW 3: Purl to 6 (6, 7, 8, 9) sts before wrapped st, wrap next st, turn.

SHORT-ROWS 4, 6, AND 8: (RS) Knit to end.

SHORT-ROW 5: Purl to 5 (6, 7, 8, 8) sts before wrapped st, wrap next st, turn.

SHORT-ROW 7: Purl to 5 (6, 7, 7, 8) sts before wrapped st, wrap next st, turn.

SHORT-ROW 9: Purl to 5 (6, 6, 7, 8) sts before wrapped st, wrap next st, turn.

SHORT-ROW 10: Knit to end.

BO all sts pwise, working wraps tog with wrapped sts as you come to them.

FRONT

Return 99 (109, 119, 129, 139) held sts to largest cir needle and, with WS facing, rejoin yarn. Shape armholes as for back—111 (121, 131, 141, 151) sts. Work even until armhole measures 1½ (2, 2½, 2, 2½)" (3.8 [5, 6.5, 5, 6.5] cm), ending with a WS row.

BEG BRIOCHE ST FRONT PANEL

NEXT ROW: (RS) K48 (53, 58, 61, 66), pm, k6 (6, 6, 8, 8), work Row 1 of Brioche st (see Stitch Guide) over 3 sts, k6 (6, 6, 8, 8), pm, knit to end.

NEXT ROW: (WS) Purl to m, sl m, p6 (6, 6, 8, 8), work Row 2 of Brioche st over 3 sts, p6 (6, 6, 8, 8), sl m, purl to end.

NEXT ROW: Knit to m, sl m, k6 (6, 6, 8, 8), work Row 3 of Brioche st over 3 sts, k6 (6, 6, 8, 8), sl m, knit to end.

Rep last 2 rows once more, then work WS row again.

NEXT ROW: (RS) Knit to m, sl m, k4 (4, 4, 6, 6), sl1yo, k1, work Row 3 of Brioche st over 3 sts, k1, sl1yo, k4 (4, 4, 6, 6), sl m, knit to end.

NEXT ROW: Purl to m, sl m, p4 (4, 4, 6, 6), work Row 2 of Brioche st over 7 sts, p4 (4, 4, 6, 6), sl m, purl to end.

NEXT ROW: Knit to m, sl m, k4 (4, 4, 6, 6), work Row 3 of Brioche st over 7 sts, k4 (4, 4, 6, 6), sl m, knit to end.

Rep last 2 rows once more, then work WS row again.

NEXT ROW: (RS) Knit to m, sl m, k2 (2, 2, 4, 4), sl1yo, k1, work Row 3 of Brioche st over 7 sts, k1, sl1yo, k2 (2, 2, 4, 4), sl m, knit to end.

NEXT ROW: Purl to m, sl m, p2 (2, 2, 4, 4), work Row 2 of Brioche st over 11 sts, p2 (2, 2, 4, 4), sl m, purl to end.

NEXT ROW: Knit to m, sl m, k2 (2, 2, 4, 4), work Row 3 of Brioche st over 11 sts, k2 (2, 2, 4, 4), sl m, knit to end.

Rep last 2 rows once more, then work WS row again.

NEXT ROW: (RS) Knit to m, sl m, k0 (0, 0, 2, 2), sl1yo, k1, work Row 3 of Brioche st over 11 sts, k1, sl1yo, k0 (0, 0, 2, 2), sl m, knit to end.

Sizes 51½ (55½)" (131 [141] cm) only

NEXT ROW: Purl to m, sl m, p2, work Row 2 of Brioche st over 15 sts, p2, sl m, purl to end.

NEXT ROW: Knit to m, sl m, k2, work Row 3 of Brioche st over 15 sts, k2, sl m, knit to end.

Rep last 2 rows once more, then work WS row again.

NEXT ROW: (RS) Knit to m, sl m, sl1yo, k1, work Row 3 of Brioche st over 15 sts, k1, sl1yo, sl m, knit to end.

All sizes

Cont in patt as established until armhole measures 4¾ (5¼, 5¾, 6½, 7¼)" (12 [13.5, 14.5, 16.5, 18.5] cm), ending with a WS row.

SHAPE NECK

NEXT ROW: (RS) K35 (40, 43, 48, 53) and place these sts on holder for left shoulder, BO 13 (13, 15, 13, 13) sts (see Notes), remove m, place center 15 (15, 15, 19, 19) sts on holder, remove m, join new yarn and BO 13 (13, 15, 13, 13) sts, knit to end—35 (40, 43, 48, 53) sts rem for right shoulder.

RIGHT SHOULDER

Purl 1 WS row.

DEC ROW: (RS) K1, ssk, knit to end—1 st dec'd.

Rep dec row every RS row 2 more times—32 (37, 40, 45, 50) sts rem.

Work even until armhole measures 6 (6½, 7, 7¾, 8½)" (15 [16.5, 18, 19.5, 21.5] cm), ending with a WS row.

Shape shoulder using short-rows, as foll:

SHORT ROW 1: (RS) Knit to last 6 (7, 7, 8, 9) sts, wrap next st, turn.

SHORT-ROWS 2, 4, 6, AND 8: (WS) Purl to end.

SHORT-ROW 3: Knit to 6 (6, 7, 8, 9) sts before wrapped st, wrap next st, turn.

SHORT-ROW 5: Knit to 5 (6, 7, 8, 8) sts before wrapped st, wrap next st, turn.

SHORT-ROW 7: Knit to 5 (6, 7, 7, 8) sts before wrapped st, wrap next st, turn.

SHORT-ROW 9: Knit to 5 (6, 6, 7, 8) sts before wrapped st, wrap next st, turn.

SHORT-ROW 10: Purl to end.

BO all sts kwise, working wraps tog with wrapped sts as you come to them.

LEFT SHOULDER

Return 35 (40, 43, 48, 53) held left shoulder sts to needle and, with WS facing, rejoin yarn. Purl 1 WS row.

DEC ROW: (RS) Knit to last 3 sts, k2tog, k1—1 st dec'd.

Rep dec row every RS row 2 more times—32 (37, 40, 45, 50) sts rem.

Work even until armhole measures 6 (6½, 7, 7¾, 8½)" (15 [16.5, 18, 19.5, 21.5] cm), ending with a RS row.

Shape shoulder using short-rows, as foll:

SHORT-ROW 1: (WS) Purl to last 6 (7, 7, 8, 9) sts, wrap next st, turn.

SHORT-ROWS 2, 4, 6, AND 8: (RS) Knit to end.

SHORT-ROW 3: Purl to 6 (6, 7, 8, 9) sts before wrapped st, wrap next st, turn.

SHORT-ROW 5: Purl to 5 (6, 7, 8, 8) sts before wrapped st, wrap next st, turn.

SHORT-ROW 7: Purl to 5 (6, 7, 7, 8) sts before wrapped st, wrap next st, turn.

SHORT-ROW 9: Purl to 5 (6, 6, 7, 8) sts before wrapped st, wrap next st, turn.

SHORT-ROW 10: Knit to end.

BO all sts pwise, working wraps tog with wrapped sts as you come to them.

SLEEVES

Sew shoulder and underarm seams. With larger dpn and RS facing, beg at underarm seam, pick up and knit 31 (34, 36, 40, 44) sts evenly along armhole edge to shoulder seam, then 31 (34, 36, 40, 44) sts to underarm seam—62 (68, 72, 80, 88) sts. Turn work WS out.

Wyb, sl 1 st from right needle to left needle. Wyf (wrapping st), sl 1 st from left needle to right needle. Pm and join in the rnd.

Knit 12 (9, 7, 6, 5) rnds.

DEC RND: K1, k2tog, knit to last 3 sts, ssk, k1—2 sts dec'd.

Rep dec rnd every 14 (11, 9, 8, 7)th rnd 3 (1, 7, 10, 1) more time(s), then every 13 (10, 8, 7, 6)th rnd 4 (9, 5, 4, 17) times—46 (46, 46, 50, 50) sts rem; sleeve measures about 15 (15½, 15½, 16, 16)" (38 [39.5, 39.5, 40.5, 40.5] cm).

Turn work RS out. Change to smaller dpn and wrap last st of rnd as before.

Knit every st tbl for 6 rnds—sleeve measures 15½ (16, 16, 16½, 16½)" (39.5 [40.5, 40.5, 42, 42] cm). BO all sts in patt.

FINISHING

Block to measurements.

COLLAR

With medium-size cir needle and RS facing, beg at center back neck, pick up and knit 35 (35, 37, 35, 35) sts evenly along left side of neck to brioche sts on holder, pm, work Row 3 of Brioche St across 15 (15, 15, 19, 19) sts, pm, pick up and knit 35 (35, 37, 35, 35) sts along right side of neck to center back neck—85 (85, 89, 89, 89) sts. Do not join.

NEXT ROW: (WS) Sl 1 pwise wyf, *k1, sl1yo; rep from * to m, sl m, work Row 2 of Brioche st to m, sl m, **sl1yo, k1; rep from ** to last st, p1.

NEXT ROW: (RS) Sl 1 pwise wyb, work Row 3 of Brioche st to last st, k1.

NEXT ROW: Sl 1 pwise wyf, work Row 2 of Brioche st to last st, p1. Rep last 2 rows until collar measures 5" (12.5 cm).

Change to largest cir needle and cont in patt until collar measures 10" (25.5 cm) ending with a RS row.

NEXT ROW: (WS) Sl 1 pwise wyf, *brk, p1; rep from * to end.

BO ALL STS AS FOLL: K1, *p1, sl left needle through front of 2 sts on right needle, k2tog tbl, k1, sl left needle through front of 2 sts on right needle, k2tog tbl; rep from * until 1 st rem on right needle; break yarn and pull through.

Sew collar seam with seam allowance on RS of garment so it will be concealed when collar is folded down.

Weave in ends.

TOPANGA
CANYON

CARDIGAN

Véronik Avery

The Topanga Canyon Cardigan is a relaxed and enveloping waterfall cardigan made for year-round wear. Let the textured front panels drape for a flowing silhouette or pin the cardigan at the shoulder for a wrapped-up look. This cardigan is worked back and forth in separate pieces and seamed.

FINISHED SIZE

17 (18½, 20, 21½, 23, 24½, 26)" (43 [47, 51, 54.5, 58.5, 62, 66] cm) back width at underarm. Cardigan shown measures 18½" (47 cm) on a model with a 34" (86.5 cm) bust.

YARN

Worsted weight (#4)

SHOWN HERE: Jo Sharp Silkroad Aran Tweed (85% wool, 10% silk, 5% cashmere; 104 yd [95 m]/1¾ oz [50 g]): #114 vermouth, 13 (14, 15, 16, 18, 19, 20) balls. Yarn distributed by Kingfisher Yarn & Fibre.

NEEDLES

Size U.S. 5 (3.75 mm): 32" circular (cir).

Size U.S. 7 (4.5 mm): 32" cir.

Adjust needle size if necessary to obtain the correct gauge.

NOTIONS

Cable needle (cn); stitch holders; tapestry needle.

GAUGE

16 sts and 27 rows = 4" (10 cm) in charted patt on larger needle; 17 sts and 25 rows = 4" (10 cm) in St st on larger needle.

NOTES

- This cardigan is worked back and forth in separate pieces and seamed. The back and front pieces are worked to the top of the shoulder, then the sts are put on holders; after seaming, the held sts are returned to the needle, and sts are picked up across the saddle shoulders in order to continue knitting the draped fronts and attached back collar.

- When beg the collar, if the last chart row worked on the back and front pieces was Row 19, 21, or 23, work through the end of the chart across all sts, then begin moss st with Row 4. If the last chart row worked was Row 1, 5, 9, 13, or 17, begin moss st with Row 1. If the last chart row worked was Row 3, 7, 11, or 15, begin moss st with Row 3.

- A cir needle is used to accommodate the large number of sts.

STITCH GUIDE

**K2, P2 RIB
(MULTIPLE OF 4 STS + 2)**

ROW 1: (RS) *K2, p2; rep from * to last 2 sts, k2.

ROW 2: (WS) *P2, k2; rep from * to last 2 sts, p2.

Rep Rows 1 and 2 for patt.

**MOSS STITCH
(EVEN NUMBER OF STS)**

ROW 1: (RS) K1, *p1, k1; rep from * to last st, k1.

ROW 2: P1, *p1, k1; rep from * to last st, p1.

ROW 3: K1, *k1, p1; rep from * to last st, k1.

ROW 4: P1, *k1, p1; rep from * to last st, p1.

Rep Rows 1–4 for patt.

INSTRUCTIONS

BACK

With smaller needle, CO 74 (78, 86, 90, 98, 102, 110) sts. Do not join.

Work in K2, P2 Rib (see Stitch Guide) for 24 rows. Change to larger needle.

NEXT ROW: (RS) K2, [k2tog] 1 (0, 1, 0, 1, 0, 1) time, knit to last 4 (2, 4, 2, 4, 2, 4) sts, [k2tog] 1 (0, 1, 0, 1, 0, 1) time, k2—72 (78, 84, 90, 96, 102, 108) sts rem.

Beg with a WS row, work Moss St Bands chart until piece measures 4¾ (4¾, 5, 5, 4¼, 4¼, 4¼)" (12 [12, 12.5, 12.5, 11, 11, 11] cm) from CO, ending with a WS row.

SHAPE WAIST

DEC ROW: (RS) K1, k2tog or p2tog as needed to maintain patt, work in patt to last 3 sts, ssk or ssp as needed to maintain patt, k1—2 sts dec'd. Rep dec row every 6 (6, 6, 6, 8, 8, 8)th row 3 more times—64 (70, 76, 82, 88, 94, 100) sts rem.

Work even until piece measures 8¾ (8¾, 9, 9, 9½, 9½, 9½)" (22 [22, 23, 23, 24, 24, 24] cm) from CO, ending with a WS row.

INC ROW: (RS) K1, M1R or M1RP as needed to maintain patt, work in patt to last st, M1L or M1LP as needed to maintain patt, k1—2 sts inc'd.

Work 11 (11, 13, 13, 13, 15, 15) rows even, ending with a WS row.

Rep inc row—68 (74, 80, 86, 92, 98, 104) sts.

Work even until piece measures 12½ (13, 13½, 13¾, 14¼, 14½, 15)" (31.5 [33, 34.5, 35, 36, 37, 38] cm) from CO, ending with a WS row.

SHAPE ARMHOLES

BO 2 (2, 3, 3, 4, 4, 5) sts at beg of next 2 rows—64 (70, 74, 80, 84, 90, 94) sts rem.

DEC ROW: (RS) K1, k2tog or p2tog as needed to maintain patt, work in patt to last 3 sts, ssk or ssp as needed to maintain patt, k1—2 sts dec'd.

Rep dec row every RS row 3 (5, 6, 7, 7, 9, 9) more times—56 (58, 60, 64, 68, 70, 74) sts rem.

Work even until armhole measures 6½ (6¾, 7¼, 7¾, 8¼, 8¾, 9¼)" (16.5 [17, 18.5, 19.5, 21, 22, 23.5] cm), ending with a WS row and making a note of last chart row worked.

SHAPE SHOULDERS

Cont in patt, BO 4 (4, 4, 5, 5, 5, 6) sts at beg of next 6 rows, then BO 6 (7, 7, 6, 7, 8, 6) sts at beg of foll 2 rows—20 (20, 22, 22, 24, 24, 26) sts rem.

Make a note of last chart row worked. Place sts on holder.

LEFT FRONT

With smaller needle, CO 94 (94, 98, 102, 106, 106, 110) sts. Do not join.

Work in K2, P2 Rib for 24 rows. Change to larger needle.

NEXT ROW: (RS) K2, [k2tog] 1 (0, 0, 1, 1, 0, 0) time, knit to last 4 (2, 2, 4, 4, 2, 2) sts, [k2tog] 1 (0, 0, 1, 1, 0, 0) time, k2—92 (94, 98, 100, 104, 106, 110) sts rem.

Beg with a WS row, work Moss St Bands chart until piece measures 4¾ (4¾, 5, 5, 4¼, 4¼, 4¼)" (12 [12, 12.5, 12.5, 11, 11, 11] cm) from CO, ending with a WS row.

SHAPE WAIST

DEC ROW: (RS) K1, k2tog or p2tog as needed to maintain patt, work in patt to end—1 st dec'd.

Rep dec row every 6 (6, 6, 6, 8, 8, 8)th row 3 more times—88 (90, 94, 96, 100, 102, 106) sts rem.

Work even until piece measures 8¾ (8¾, 9, 9, 9½, 9½, 9½)" (22 [22, 23, 23, 24, 24, 24] cm) from CO, ending with a WS row.

INC ROW: (RS) K1, M1R or M1RP as needed to maintain patt, work in patt to end—1 st inc'd.

Work 11 (11, 13, 13, 13, 15, 15) rows even, ending with a WS row.

Rep inc row—90 (92, 96, 98, 102, 104, 108) sts.

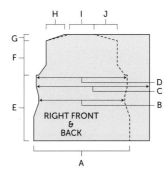

RIGHT FRONT & BACK

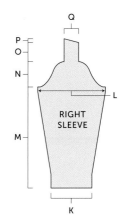

RIGHT SLEEVE

A: 18 (19½, 21, 22½, 24, 25½, 27)" (45.5 [49.5, 53.5, 57, 61, 65, 68.5] cm)

B: 16 (17½, 19, 20½, 22, 23½, 25)" (40.5 [44.5, 48.5, 52, 56, 59.5, 63.5] cm)

C: 22½ (23, 24, 24½, 25½, 26, 27)" (57 [58.5, 61, 62, 65, 65, 66, 68.5] cm)

D: 17 (18½, 20, 21½, 23, 24½, 26)" (43 [47, 51, 57, 58.5, 62, 66] cm)

E: 12½ (13, 13½, 13¾, 14¼, 14½, 15)" (31.5 [33, 34.5, 35, 36, 37, 38] cm)

F: 6½ (6¾, 7¼, 7¾, 8¼, 8¾, 9¼)" (16.5 [17, 18.5, 19.5, 21, 22, 23.5] cm)

G: 1¼" (3.2 cm)

H: 3½ (3¾, 3¾, 4¼, 4½, 4¾, 5)" (9 [9.5, 9.5, 11, 11.5, 12, 12.5] cm)

I: 5 (5, 5½, 5½, 6, 6, 6½)" (12.5 [12.5, 14, 14, 15, 15, 16.5] cm)

J: 4½ (4¾, 4¾, 5¼, 5½, 5¾, 6)" (11.5 [12, 12, 13.5, 14, 14.5, 15] cm)

K: 8 (8½, 9, 9½, 10, 10¼, 10¾)" (20.5 [21.5, 23, 2425.5, 26, 27.5] cm)

L: 12¾ (13¾, 14½, 15½, 16½, 17½, 18¼)" (32 [35, 37, 39.5, 42, 44.5, 46.5] cm)

M: 20 (20, 20, 20¼, 20¼, 20¼, 20¾)" (51 [51, 51, 51.5, 51.5, 51.5, 52.5] cm)

N: 4¾ (5, 5¾, 6, 6¾, 7, 7¾)" (12 [12.5, 14.5, 15, 17, 18, 19.5] cm)

O: 3¼ (3¾, 3¾, 4, 4¼, 4¾, 5)" (8.5 [9.5, 9.5, 10, 11, 12, 12.5] cm)

P: ¾" (2 cm)

Q: 3¼" (8.5 cm)

MOSS STITCH BANDS

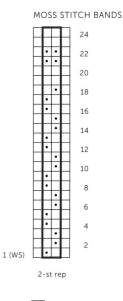

1 (WS)

2-st rep

 k on RS; p on WS

 p on RS; k on WS

pattern repeat

Work even until piece measures 12½ (13, 13½, 13¾, 14¼, 14½, 15)" (31.5 [33, 34.5, 35, 36, 37, 38] cm) from CO, ending with a WS row.

SHAPE ARMHOLE

NEXT ROW: (RS) BO 2 (2, 3, 3, 4, 4, 5) sts, work to end—88 (90, 93, 95, 98, 100, 103) sts rem.

Work 1 WS row.

DEC ROW: (RS) K1, k2tog or p2tog as needed to maintain patt, work in patt to end—1 st dec'd.

Rep dec row every RS row 3 (5, 6, 7, 7, 9, 9) more times—84 (84, 86, 87, 90, 90, 93) sts rem.

Work even until armhole measures 6½ (6¾, 7¼, 7¾, 8¼, 8¾, 9¼)" (16.5 [17, 18.5, 19.5, 21, 22, 23.5] cm), ending with same chart row as back before shoulder.

SHAPE SHOULDER

At beg of RS rows, BO 3 (3, 3, 4, 4, 4, 4) sts 3 times, then BO 5 (6, 6, 5, 6, 7, 8) sts once—70 (69, 71, 70, 72, 71, 73) sts rem. Work 1 WS row. Place sts on holder.

RIGHT FRONT

With smaller needle, CO 94 (94, 98, 102, 106, 106, 110) sts. Do not join.

Work in K2, P2 Rib for 24 rows. Change to larger needle.

NEXT ROW: (RS) K2, [k2tog] 1 (0, 0, 1, 1, 0, 0) time, knit to last 4 (2, 2, 4, 4, 2, 2) sts, [k2tog] 1 (0, 0, 1, 1, 0, 0) time, k2—92 (94, 98, 100, 104, 106, 110) sts rem.

Beg with a WS row, work Moss St Bands chart until piece measures 4¾ (4¾, 5, 5, 4¼, 4¼, 4¼)" (12 [12, 12.5, 12.5, 11, 11, 11] cm) from CO, ending with a WS row.

SHAPE WAIST

DEC ROW: (RS) Work in patt to last 3 sts, ssk or ssp as needed to maintain patt, k1—1 st dec'd.

Rep dec row every 6 (6, 6, 6, 8, 8, 8)th row 3 more times—88 (90, 94, 96, 100, 102, 106) sts rem.

Work even until piece measures 8¾ (8¾, 9, 9, 9½, 9½, 9½)" (22 [22, 23, 23, 24, 24, 24] cm) from CO, ending with a WS row.

INC ROW: (RS) Work in patt to last st, M1L or M1LP as needed to maintain patt, k1—1 st inc'd.

Work 11 (11, 13, 13, 13, 15, 15) rows even, ending with a WS row.

Rep inc row—90 (92, 96, 98, 102, 104, 108) sts.

Work even until piece measures 12½ (13, 13½, 13¾, 14¼, 14½, 15)" (31.5 [33, 34.5, 35, 36, 37, 38] cm) from CO, ending with a RS row.

SHAPE ARMHOLE

NEXT ROW: (WS) BO 2 (2, 3, 3, 4, 4, 5) sts, work to end—88 (90, 93, 95, 98, 100, 103) sts rem.

DEC ROW: (RS) Work in patt to last 3 sts, ssk or ssp as needed to maintain patt, k1—1 st dec'd.

Rep dec row every RS row 3 (5, 6, 7, 7, 9, 9) more times—84 (84, 86, 87, 90, 90, 93) sts rem.

Work even until armhole measures 6½ (6¾, 7¼, 7¾, 8¼, 8¾, 9¼)" (16.5 [17, 18.5, 19.5, 21, 22, 23.5] cm), ending 1 row after chart row on back before shoulder.

SHAPE SHOULDER

At beg of WS rows, BO 3 (3, 3, 4, 4, 4, 4) sts 3 times, then BO 5 (6, 6, 5, 6, 7, 8) sts once—70 (69, 71, 70, 72, 71, 73) sts rem. Place sts on holder.

LEFT SLEEVE

With larger needle, CO 34 (36, 38, 40, 42, 44, 46) sts. Do not join. Work in St st for 4¼ (2¾, 4¾, 3¾, 2½, 5½, 5)" (11.5 [7, 12, 9.5, 9.5, 6.5, 14, 12.5] cm), ending with a WS row.

INC ROW: (RS) K2, M1R, knit to last 2 sts, M1L, k2—2 sts inc'd.

Rep inc row every 10 (10, 8, 8, 8, 6, 6)th row 9 (10, 11, 12, 13, 14, 15) more times—54 (58, 62, 66, 70, 74, 78) sts.

Work even until piece measures 20 (20, 20, 20¼, 20¼, 20¼, 20¾)" (51 [51, 51, 51.5, 51.5, 51.5, 52.5] cm) from CO, ending with a WS row.

SHAPE CAP

BO 2 (2, 3, 3, 4, 4, 5) sts at beg of next 2 rows—50 (54, 56, 60, 62, 66, 68) sts rem.

DEC ROW: (RS) K2, sl 2 sts onto cn, hold cn parallel to and behind left needle, [insert right needle into first st on left needle and first st on cn and k2tog] 2 times, knit to last 6 sts, sl 2 sts onto cn, hold cn parallel to and in front of left needle, [insert right needle into first st on cn and first st on left needle and k2tog] 2 times, k2—4 sts dec'd.

Rep dec row every RS row 1 (2, 1, 2, 1, 2, 1) more time(s)—42 (42, 48, 48, 54, 54, 60) sts rem. Work 1 WS row.

DEC ROW: (RS) K2, k2tog, knit to last 4 sts, ssk, k2—2 sts dec'd. Rep dec row every RS row 9 (9, 12, 12, 15, 15, 18) more times—22 sts rem.

Work 1 WS row.

BO 2 sts at beg of next 4 rows—14 sts rem.

SADDLE

Work 21 (23, 23, 25, 27, 29, 31) rows even, ending with a RS row.

SHAPE NECK: At beg of WS rows, BO 5 sts 2 times—4 sts rem. Work 1 RS row. BO all sts.

RIGHT SLEEVE

Work as for left sleeve to saddle.

SADDLE

Work 22 (24, 24, 26, 28, 30, 32) rows even, ending with a WS row.

SEWN BIND-OFF

Cut the yarn 3 times the width of the knitting to be bound off and thread onto a tapestry needle. Working from right to left, *insert tapestry needle pwise (from right to left) through first 2 sts **(Figure 1)** and pull the yarn through, then bring needle kwise (from left to right) through the first st **(Figure 2),** pull the yarn through, and remove this st from the knitting needle. Repeat from *.

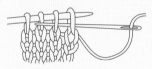

FIGURE 1

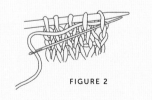

FIGURE 2

SHAPE NECK: At beg of RS rows, BO 5 sts 2 times—4 sts rem. Work 1 WS row. BO all sts.

FINISHING

Weave in ends. Block pieces to measurements.

Sew sleeve caps into armholes and saddles to shoulders. Sew sleeve and side seams.

COLLAR

Return held sts to smaller needle. With larger needle and RS facing, work Moss st (see Stitch Guide) as established (see Notes) across 70 (69, 71, 70, 72, 71, 73) right front sts, pick up and knit 12 sts along right saddle, work Moss st as established across 20 (20, 22, 22, 24, 24, 26) back sts, pick up and knit 12 sts along left saddle, work Moss st as established across 70 (69, 71, 70, 72, 71, 73) left front sts—184 (182, 188, 186, 192, 190, 196) sts total.

Cont in patt across all sts, work 12 rows even, ending with a RS row. Purl 1 WS row. Knit 2 rows. With RS facing, BO all sts pwise.

LEFT FRONT BAND

With smaller needle and RS facing, beg at top of left front, pick up and knit 106 (110, 114, 118, 122, 126, 130) sts evenly spaced along left front selvedge edge.

Knit 1 WS row.

NEXT ROW: (RS) K4, *p2, k2; rep from * to last 2 sts, k2.

NEXT ROW: (WS) K2, *p2, k2; rep from * to end.

Rep last 2 rows 6 more times. Using the sewn method (see Sidebar), BO all sts.

RIGHT FRONT BAND

With smaller needle and RS facing, beg at right front lower edge, pick up and knit 106 (110, 114, 118, 122, 126, 130) sts evenly spaced along right front selvedge edge.

Complete as for left front band.

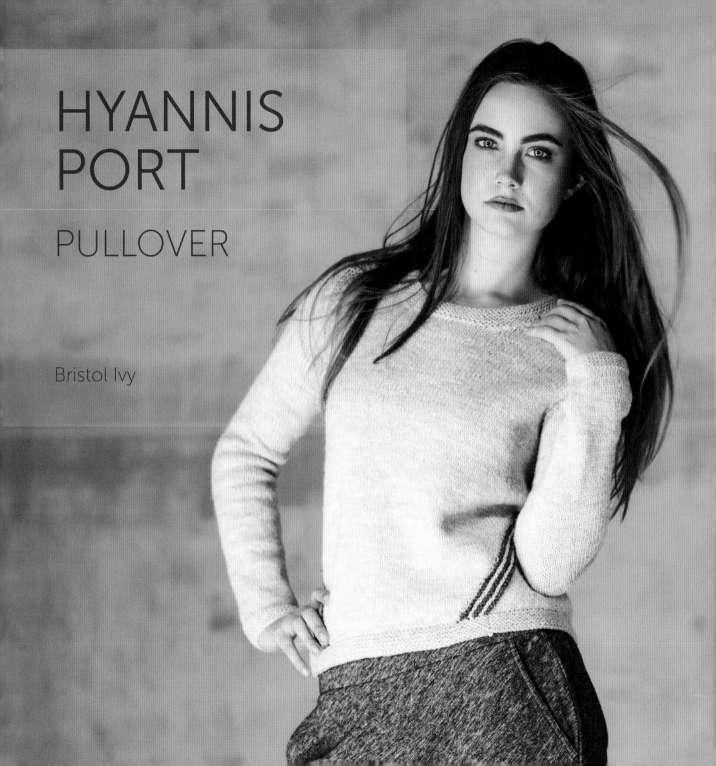

HYANNIS PORT

PULLOVER

Bristol Ivy

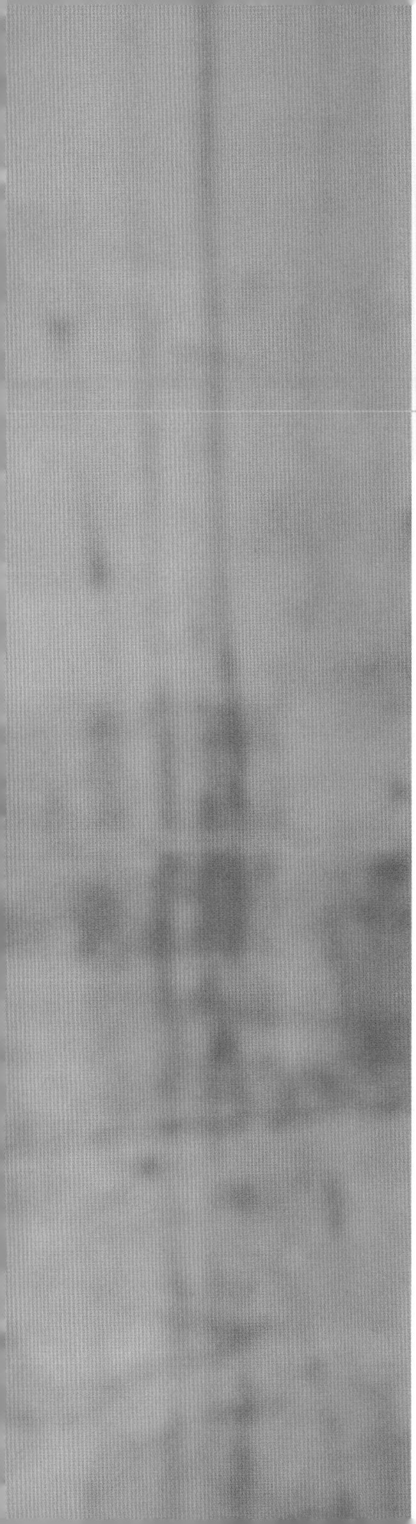

Intriguing geometric construction and well-placed stripes draw the eye to the Hyannis Port Pullover. The natural colors of this DK weight wool yarn let the compelling short-rows and stitch work shine.

FINISHED SIZE

32½ (36, 39¾, 43½, 47½, 51¼, 55, 57)" (82.5 [91.5, 101, 110.5, 120.5, 130, 139.5, 145] cm) bust circumference. Pullover shown measures 36" (91.5 cm); modeled with 1" (2.5 cm) of positive ease.

YARN

DK weight (#3)

SHOWN HERE: Bare Naked Wools Kent DK (60% merino, 40% Romney; 300 yd [274 m]/4 oz [115 g]): white sand (MC), 4 (4, 4, 5, 5, 5, 6, 6) skeins; mussel shell (CC), 1 skein.

NEEDLES

Size U.S. 7 (4.5 mm): 32" and 16" circular (cir) and set of double-pointed (dpn).

Size U.S. 8 (5 mm): 32" cir.

Adjust needle size if necessary to obtain the correct gauge.

NOTIONS

Markers (m); removable m; stitch holders; tapestry needle.

GAUGE

19½ sts and 29 rows = 4" (10 cm) in St st on larger needle.

NOTES

• This sweater is worked in sections. First, the sleeves are worked in the round to the underarm and set aside. The back curved hem piece is worked and bound off. Front sts are picked up from each end of back piece, with extra sts cast on at center front, then the lower body is joined in the round by working the front wedge in short-rows. The rest of the lower body and yoke is worked upward with raglan shaping. The neckband and hem are added during finishing.

STITCH GUIDE

BACKWARD YO (BYO):
Bring yarn over right needle from back to front, then between needles to back.

INSTRUCTIONS

SLEEVES

With MC, smaller dpn, and using the long-tail method, CO 40 (40, 40, 40, 40, 42, 42, 42) sts. Place marker (pm) and join in the rnd.

[Knit 1 rnd, purl 1 rnd] 5 times.

Change to larger dpn and St st. Knit 1 rnd.

INC RND: K1, M1L, knit to last st, M1R, k1—2 sts inc'd.

Rep inc rnd every 18 (14, 12, 10, 8, 8, 6, 6)th rnd 6 (8, 7, 6, 11, 2, 18, 12) more times, then every 0 (0, 10, 8, 6, 6, 4, 4)th rnd 0 (0, 3, 7, 5, 17, 3, 12) times—54 (58, 62, 68, 74, 82, 86, 92) sts.

Work even until piece measures 19" (48.5 cm) from CO, ending 2 (3, 4, 4, 5, 5, 6, 6) sts before end of rnd on last rnd.

NEXT RND: BO 4 (6, 8, 8, 10, 10, 12, 12) sts, removing m, knit to end—50 (52, 54, 60, 64, 72, 74, 80) sts rem. Place sts on holder and set aside.

BACK CURVED HEM

With MC, larger cir needle, and using the long-tail method, CO 4 (4, 16, 8, 20, 4, 20, 36) sts. Do not join.

NEXT ROW: (WS) P1, pm, purl to last st, pm, p1.

Sizes 32½ (36, 51¼)" (82.5 [91.5, 130] cm) only

NEXT ROW: (RS) K1, yo, sl m, k1, LLI, RLI, k1, sl m, byo (see Stitch Guide), k1—8 sts.

NEXT ROW: (WS) P1, purl byo tfl to twist it, sl m, purl to m, sl m, purl yo tbl to twist it, p1.

Sizes 39¾ (43½, 47½, 55, 57)" (101 [110.5, 120.5, 139.5, 145] cm) only

NEXT ROW: (RS) K1, yo, sl m, k1, yo, knit to 1 st before m, byo (see Stitch Guide), k1, sl m, byo, k1—20 (12, 24, 24, 40) sts.

NEXT ROW: (WS) P1, purl byo tfl to twist it, sl m, p1, purl byo tfl, purl to 2 sts before m, purl yo tbl to twist it, p1, sl m, purl yo tbl, p1.

All sizes

INC ROW: (RS) K1, yo, knit to m, sl m, k1, yo, knit to 1 st before m, byo, k1, sl m, knit to last st, byo, k1—4 sts inc'd.

NEXT ROW: (WS) P1, purl byo tfl, purl to m, sl m, p1, purl byo tfl, purl to 2 sts before m, purl yo tbl, p1, sl m, purl to last 2 sts, purl yo tbl, p1.

Rep last 2 rows 42 (42, 44, 44, 45, 45, 45, 45) more times—180 (180, 200, 192, 208, 192, 208, 224) sts.

Join CC.

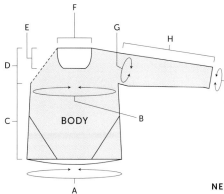

A: 34¾ (38½, 42¾, 46½, 50¼, 54, 58, 61¾)" (88.5 [98, 108.5, 118, 127.5, 137, 147.5, 157] cm)

B: 32½ (36, 39¾, 43½, 47½, 51¼, 55, 57)" (82.5 [91.5, 101, 110.5, 120.5, 127.5, 139.5, 145] cm)

C: 15" (38 cm)

D: 6 (6¾, 7, 7½, 8, 8½, 8¾, 9½)" (15 [17, 18, 19, 20.5, 52, 22, 24] cm)

E: 3¾" (9.5 cm)

F: 6¼ (7, 7¾, 7½, 7½, 6½, 7½, 7½)" (16 [18, 19.5, 19, 19, 16.5, 19, 19] cm)

G: 11 (12, 12¾, 14, 15¼, 16¾, 17¾, 18¾)" (28 [30.5, 32, 35.5, 38.5, 42.5, 45, 47.5] cm)

H: 19" (48.5 cm)

I: 8¼ (8¼, 8¼, 8¼, 8¼, 8½, 8½, 8½)" (21 [21, 21, 21, 21, 21.5, 21.5, 21.5] cm)

NEXT ROW: (RS) With CC, k1, yo, knit to m, sl m, k1, yo, knit to 1 st before m, byo, k1, sl m, knit to last st, byo, k1—4 sts inc'd.

NEXT ROW: (WS) With CC, k1, knit byo tfl, knit to m, sl m, k1, knit byo tfl, knit to 2 sts before m, knit yo tbl, k1, sl m, knit to last 2 sts, knit yo tbl, k1.

With MC, rep last 2 rows—4 sts inc'd.

Rep last 4 rows once more, then rep 2 CC rows once more—200 (200, 220, 212, 228, 212, 228, 244) sts: 50 (50, 52, 52, 53, 53, 53, 53) sts at each side, and 100 (100, 116, 108, 122, 106, 122, 138) center sts.

With CC, BO all sts, using the sewn BO method.

BODY

Lay back curved hem on a flat surface with RS facing, with BO edge of center section across top, and BO edge of each side sloping down from top edge.

With MC, larger cir needle, and using the long-tail method, CO 16 (34, 40, 64, 70, 100, 108, 114) sts for center front. Do not turn work.

With same needle and yarn, and picking up at a rate of about 7 sts for every 10 BO sts, pm, pick up and knit 36 (36, 36, 36, 38, 38, 37, 38) sts from BO edge of back curved hem along first side section, 70 (70, 82, 76, 86, 74, 86, 96) sts across center section, and 36 (36, 36, 36, 38, 38, 37, 38) sts along BO edge of 2nd side section, then join in the rnd, pm, knit first 8 (17, 20, 32, 35, 50, 54, 57) CO sts, pm for end of rnd at center front—158 (176, 194, 212, 232, 250, 268, 286) sts total: 142 (142, 154, 148, 162, 150, 160, 172) picked-up sts, and 8 (17, 20, 32, 35, 50, 54, 57) front sts each side of m at center front.

Work short-rows to fill in space between ends of back curved hem using the Japanese short-row method as foll:

SHORT-ROW 1: (RS) Knit to m, remove m, k1, turn work, sl 1 pwise wyf, place removable m on working yarn.

SHORT-ROW 2: (WS) Purl to rnd m, sl m, purl to m, remove m, p1, turn work, sl 1 pwise wyb, place removable m on working yarn.

SHORT-ROW 3: Knit to gap, pull up on m and place loop on left needle, making sure it isn't twisted, remove m, k2tog, turn work, sl 1 pwise wyf, place removable m on working yarn.

SHORT-ROW 4: Purl to gap, sl 1 pwise wyf, pull up on m and place loop on left needle, making sure it isn't twisted, remove m, sl st from right needle back to left needle, p2tog, turn work, sl 1 pwise wyb, place removable m on working yarn.

Rep last 2 short-rows 35 (35, 39, 36, 39, 35, 40, 36) more times.

SHORT-ROW 5: Knit to gap, pull up on m and place loop on left needle, making sure it isn't twisted, remove m, k2tog, k1, turn work, sl 1 pwise wyf, place removable m on working yarn.

SHORT-ROW 6: Purl to gap, sl 1 pwise wyf, pull up on m and place loop on left needle, making sure it isn't twisted, remove m, sl st from right needle back to left needle, p2tog, p1, turn work, sl 1 pwise wyb, place removable m on working yarn.

Rep last 2 short-rows 4 (4, 3, 5, 5, 4, 4, 5) more times.

SHORT-ROW 7: Knit to gap, pull up on m and place loop on left needle, making sure it isn't twisted, remove m, k2tog, k3, turn work, sl 1 pwise wyf, place removable m on working yarn.

SHORT-ROW 8: Purl to gap, sl 1 pwise wyf, pull up on m and place loop on left needle, making sure it isn't twisted, remove m, sl st from right needle back to left needle, p2tog, p3, turn work, sl 1 pwise wyb, place removable m on working yarn.

Rep last 2 short-rows 3 (3, 4, 3, 4, 4, 4, 6) more times—16 center back sts rem between last pair of gaps.

NEXT RND: Knit to gap, pull up on m and place loop on left needle, making sure it isn't twisted, remove m, k2tog, knit to 1 st before next gap, sl 1 pwise wyb, pull up on m and place loop on left needle, making sure it isn't twisted, remove m, sl st from right needle back to left needle, ssk, knit to rnd m at center front—piece measures 13 (13, 14, 13½, 14½, 13¼, 14½, 14¼)" (33 [33, 35.5, 34.5, 37, 33.5, 37, 36] cm) from CO at center front and

1" (2.5 cm) to 1½" (3.8 cm) longer at center back.

Work even until piece measures 15" (38 cm) from CO at center front.

DIVIDE FOR FRONT AND BACK

NEXT RND: K38 (41, 45, 49, 53, 58, 61, 66) right front sts, BO 4 (6, 8, 8, 10, 10, 12, 12) sts for right underarm, k74 (82, 88, 98, 106, 114, 122, 130) back sts, BO 4 (6, 8, 8, 10, 10, 12, 12) sts for left underarm, knit to m at center front and stop; do not break yarn—74 (82, 88, 98, 106, 114, 122, 130) back sts, and 76 (82, 90, 98, 106, 116, 122, 132) front sts rem.

YOKE

JOIN BODY AND SLEEVES

NEXT RND: K38 (41, 45, 49, 53, 58, 61, 66) right front sts, pm, k50 (52, 54, 60, 64, 72, 74, 80) right sleeve sts from holder, pm, k74 (82, 88, 98, 106, 114, 122, 130) back sts, pm, k50 (52, 54, 60, 64, 72, 74, 80) left sleeve sts from holder, pm, k38 (41, 45, 49, 53, 58, 61, 66) left front sts—250 (268, 286, 316, 340, 374, 392, 422) sts total.

Sizes 43½ (47½, 51¼, 55, 57)" (110.5, [120.5, 130, 139.5, 145] cm) only

DEC RND: 1 *Knit to 3 sts before m, ssk, k1, sl m, knit to m, sl m, k1, k2tog; rep from * once more, knit to end—4 sts dec'd.

DEC RND 2: *Knit to 3 sts before m, ssk, p1, sl m, k2tog, knit to 2 sts before m, ssk, sl m, p1, k2tog; rep from * once more, knit to end—8 sts dec'd.

Rep last 2 rnds 3 (6, 10, 11, 12) more times—268 (256, 242, 248, 266) sts rem: 82 (78, 72, 74, 80) front sts, 82 (78, 70, 74, 78) back sts, and 52 (50, 50, 50, 54) sts each sleeve. Knit 1 rnd.

All sizes

DEC RND: *Knit to 3 sts before m, ssk, p1, sl m, k2tog, knit to 2 sts before m, ssk, sl m, p1, k2tog; rep from * once more, knit to end—8 sts dec'd.

NEXT RND: Knit.

Rep last 2 rnds 7 (9, 10, 8, 6, 4, 4, 6) more times, ending last rnd 8 (8, 10, 11, 11, 11, 12, 12) sts before rnd m at center front—186 (188, 198, 196, 200, 202, 208, 210) sts rem: 60 (62, 68, 64, 64, 62, 64, 66) front sts, 58 (62, 66, 64, 64, 60, 64, 64) back sts, and 34 (32, 32, 34, 36, 40, 40, 40) sleeve sts; yoke measures 2¼ (3, 3¼, 3¾, 4¼, 4¾, 5, 5¾)" (5.5 [7.5, 8.5, 9.5, 11, 11, 12, 12.5, 14.5]cm) from underarm.

SHAPE FRONT NECK

Beg working back and forth in rows.

NEXT ROW: (RS) BO 16 (16, 20, 22, 22, 22, 24, 24) sts (removing rnd m), *knit to 3 sts before m, ssk, p1 sl m, k2tog, knit to 2 sts before m, ssk, sl m, p1, k2tog; rep from * once more, knit to gap at center front—162 (164, 170, 166, 170, 172, 176, 178) sts: 21 (22, 23, 20, 20, 19, 19, 20) sts each front, 56 (60, 64, 62, 62, 58, 62, 62) back sts, and 32 (30, 30, 32, 34, 38, 38, 38) sts each sleeve.

NEXT ROW: (WS) P1, p2tog, purl to last 3 sts, ssp, p1—2 sts dec'd: 1 st each neck edge.

NECK AND RAGLAN DEC ROW: (RS) K1, ssk, *knit to 3 sts before m, ssk, p1, sl m, k2tog, knit to 2 sts before m, ssk, sl m, p1, k2tog; rep from * once more, knit to last 3 sts, k2tog, k1—10 sts dec'd: 2 sts each for fronts, back, and sleeves.

NEXT ROW: (WS) Purl. Rep last 2 rows 2 (2, 2, 1, 1, 1, 1, 2) more time(s)—130 (132, 138, 144, 148, 150, 154, 146) sts: 14 (15, 16, 15, 15, 14, 14, 13) sts each front, 50 (54, 58, 58, 58, 54, 58, 56) back sts, and 26 (24, 24, 28, 30, 34, 34, 32) sts each sleeve.

RAGLAN DEC ROW: (RS) *Knit to 3 sts before m, ssk, p1, sl m, k2tog, knit to 2 sts before m, ssk, sl m, p1, k2tog; rep from * once more, knit to end—8 sts dec'd: 1 st each front, 2 sts each for back and sleeves.

NEXT ROW: (WS) Purl.

NEXT ROW: Rep neck and raglan dec row—10 sts dec'd.

NEXT ROW: Purl.

Rep last 4 rows 0 (1, 2, 0, 0, 0, 0, 0) more time(s)—112 (96, 84, 126, 130, 132, 136, 128) sts rem: 11 (9, 7, 12, 12, 11, 11, 10) sts each front, 46 (46, 46, 54, 54, 50, 54, 52) back sts, and 22 (16, 12, 24, 26, 30, 30, 28) sts each sleeve.

NEXT ROW: (RS) Work raglan dec row—8 sts dec'd.

NEXT ROW: (WS) Purl. Rep last 2 rows 7 (5, 3, 8, 8, 8, 8, 7) more times—48 (48, 52, 54, 58, 60, 64, 64) sts rem: 3 (3, 3, 3, 3, 2, 2, 2) sts each front, 30 (34, 38, 36, 36, 32, 36, 36) back sts, and 6 (4, 4, 6, 8, 12, 12, 12) sts each sleeve; yoke measures 6 (6¾, 7, 7½, 8, 8½, 8¾, 9½)" (15 [17, 18, 19, 20.5, 21.5, 22, 24] cm). BO all sts.

FINISHING

Block to measurements; lower body edging is not shown on schematic and will add about 1" (2.5 cm) to total length after finishing.

NECKBAND

With MC, smaller, shorter cir needle, and RS facing, beg at right back raglan, pick up and knit 30 (34, 38, 36, 36, 32, 36, 36) sts along back neck, 6 (4, 4, 6, 8, 12, 12, 12) sts across top of left sleeve, 18 sts along left neck, 16 (16, 20, 22, 22, 22, 24, 24) sts across center front, 18 sts along right neck, and 6 (4, 4, 6, 8, 12, 12, 12) sts across top of right sleeve—94 (94, 102, 106, 110, 114, 120, 120) sts.

Pm and join in the rnd.

[Purl 1 rnd, knit 1 rnd] 4 times, purl 1 rnd.

BO all sts as foll: Ssk, *sl 1 kwise, complete ssk; rep from * to end. Fasten off last st.

LOWER BODY EDGING

Hold garment upside down, with RS of front facing, and lower edge of body at top. Find CC garter stripes at lower left front and join MC to body to left of stripes.

With smaller 32" cir needle, pick up and knit 60 (60, 62, 62, 64, 64, 64, 64) sts along first side section of back curved hem (about 2 sts for every 3 rows), 4 (4, 16, 8, 20, 4, 20, 36) sts across center CO sts, 60 (60, 62, 62, 64, 64, 64, 64) sts along 2nd side section (about 2 sts for every 3 rows), 5 sts along edge of garter stripes, 16 (34, 40, 64, 70, 100, 108, 114) sts across center front CO, and 5 sts along edge of garter stripes—150 (168, 190, 206, 228, 242, 266, 288) sts.

Pm and join in the rnd. [Purl 1 rnd, knit 1 rnd] 4 times, purl 1 rnd.

BO all sts as for neckband. Weave in ends.

AVILA

TEE

Amanda Bell

Flowing, simple, and wearable, the Avila Tee is a casual but elegant top for the modern woman. The waterfall side panels are made after the fabric is complete with a drop-stitch technique that looks complicated but is simple enough for novice knitters to create. This tee is worked back and forth in two pieces and seamed.

FINISHED SIZE

35½ (39½, 43½, 47½, 51½)" (90 [100.5, 110.5, 120.5, 131] cm) bust circumference. Tee shown measures 35½" (90 cm); modeled with 1½" (3.8 cm) of positive ease.

YARN

Sportweight (#2)

SHOWN HERE: Manos del Uruguay Milo (65% merino wool, 35% linen; 380 yd [350 m]/3½ oz [100 g]): #i2545 indigo, 3 (4, 4, 5, 5) skeins. Yarn distributed by Fairmount Fibers.

NEEDLES

Size U.S. 6 (4 mm): 24" circular (cir).

Size U.S. 5 (3.75 mm): 16" and 24" cir.

Adjust needle size if necessary to obtain the correct gauge.

NOTIONS

Markers (m); stitch holders; tapestry needle.

GAUGE

24½ sts and 34 rows = 4" (10 cm) in St st on smaller needle.

22 sts and 32 rows = 4" (10 cm) in St st on larger needle.

NOTES

- This tee is worked back and forth in two pieces and seamed. Each piece is cast on provisionally at the bustline and worked upward to the shoulders with integrated cap sleeves. Sts are then picked up from the provisional cast-on, and the lower body is worked to the bottom hem with drop-st side panels.

FRONT

UPPER BODY

With smaller 24" needle, and using a provisional method, CO 109 (121, 133, 145, 157) sts. Do not join.

Knit 2 rows.

Beg with a RS row, work in St st until piece measures 2 (2, 2, 1½, 1½)" (5 [5, 5, 3.8, 3.8] cm) from CO, ending with a WS row.

NEXT ROW: (RS) Knit to end, place marker (pm) for sleeve, then using the backward-loop method, CO 9 sts—118 (130, 142, 154, 166) sts.

NEXT ROW: (WS) Purl to end, pm for sleeve, CO 9 sts—127 (139, 151, 163, 175) sts.

NEXT ROW: Sl 1 pwise wyf, p2, knit to last 3 sts, p3.

NEXT ROW: Sl 1 pwise wyb, k2, purl to last 3 sts, k3.

Rep last 2 rows 2 more times.

INC ROW: (RS) Work in patt to m, M1R, sl m, knit to m, sl m, M1L, work in patt to end—2 sts inc'd.

Rep inc row every 8th row 5 (5, 6, 4, 5) more times, then every 6th row 0 (0, 0, 3, 2) times—139 (151, 165, 179, 191) sts: 15 (15, 16, 17, 17) sts for each sleeve and 109 (121, 133, 145, 157) body sts.

Removing sleeve m on next row as you come to them, work even if necessary until piece measures 6 (6½, 7, 7, 7½)" (16 [16.5, 18, 18, 19] cm) from CO, ending with a WS row.

SHAPE NECK

NEXT ROW: (RS) Work 49 (55, 62, 69, 75) sts in patt and place sts just worked on holder for left shoulder, BO 41 sts, work in patt to end—49 (55, 62, 69, 75) sts rem for right shoulder.

RIGHT SHOULDER

DEC ROW: (WS) Work in patt to last 3 sts, ssp, p1—1 st dec'd.

DEC ROW: (RS) K1, ssk, work in patt to end—1 st dec'd.

Rep dec row every RS row 5 more times, then every 4th row 2 times—40 (46, 53, 60, 66) sts rem.

Work even until armhole measures 7 (7½, 8, 8½, 9)" (18 [19, 20.5, 21.5, 23] cm) from sleeve CO, ending with a WS row.

Shape shoulder using short-rows as foll:

SHORT-ROW 1: (RS) Work to last 5 (6, 7, 8, 9) sts, wrap next st, turn.

SHORT-ROW 2 AND ALL WS SHORT-ROWS: Purl to end.

SHORT-ROWS 3, 5, AND 7: Work to 5 (6, 7, 8, 9) sts before wrapped st, wrap next st, turn.

SHORT-ROW 9: Knit to 10 (11, 12, 14, 15) sts before wrapped st, wrap next st, turn.

NEXT ROW: (WS) Purl to end. BO all sts, working wraps tog with wrapped sts.

LEFT SHOULDER

Return 49 (55, 62, 69, 75) left shoulder sts to needle and, with WS facing, rejoin yarn.

DEC ROW: (WS) P1, p2tog, work in patt to end—1 st dec'd.

DEC ROW: (RS) Work in patt to last 3 sts, k2tog, k1—1 st dec'd.

Rep dec row every RS row 5 more times, then every 4th row 2 times—40 (46, 53, 60, 66) sts rem.

Work even until armhole measures 7 (7½, 8, 8½, 9)" (18 [19, 20.5, 21.5, 23] cm) from sleeve CO, ending with a RS row. Shape shoulder using short-rows as foll:

SHORT-ROW 1: (WS) Purl to last 5 (6, 7, 8, 9) sts, wrap next st, turn.

SHORT-ROW 2 AND ALL RS SHORT-ROWS: Knit to end.

SHORT-ROWS 3, 5, AND 7: Purl to 5 (6, 7, 8, 9) sts before wrapped st, wrap next st, turn.

SHORT-ROW 9: Purl to 10 (11, 12, 14, 15) sts before wrapped st, wrap next st, turn.

NEXT ROW: (RS) Knit to end.

BO all sts, working wraps tog with wrapped sts.

LOWER BODY

With larger 24" needle and using the backward-loop method, CO 13 sts, pm, remove waste yarn from provisional CO and place 108 (120, 132, 144, 156) sts on left needle, then with RS facing, knit across CO sts, pm, CO 13 sts—134 (146, 158, 170, 182) sts.

NEXT ROW: (WS) Sl 1 pwise wyb, k2, [p1tbl, yo, p1tbl, p1] 3 times, p1tbl, sl m, purl to m, sl m, p1tbl, [p1, p1tbl, yo, p1tbl] 3 times, k3—140 (152, 164, 176, 188) sts total and 16 sts each side panel.

NEXT ROW: Sl 1 pwise wyf, p2, [k1tbl, p1, k1tbl, k1] 3 times, k1tbl, sl m, knit to m, sl m, k1tbl, [k1, k1tbl, p1, k1tbl] 3 times, p3.

NEXT ROW: Sl 1 pwise wyb, k2, [p1tbl, k1, p1tbl, p1] 3 times, p1tbl, sl m, purl to m, sl m, p1tbl, [p1, p1tbl, k1, p1tbl] 3 times, k3. Rep last 2 rows 5 more times.

SHAPE SIDES

ROW 1: (RS) Sl 1 pwise wyf, p2, *k1tbl, p1, k1tbl, k1; rep from * to 1 st before m, k1tbl, yo, M1R, sl m, knit to m, sl m, M1L, yo, k1tbl, **k1, k1tbl, p1, k1tbl; rep from ** to last 3 sts, p3—4 sts inc'd: 2 sts each side panel.

ROW 2: (WS) Sl 1 pwise wyb, k2, *p1tbl, k1, p1tbl, p1; rep from * to 3 sts before m, p1tbl, k1, p1tbl, sl m, purl to m, sl m, p1tbl, k1, p1tbl, **p1, p1tbl, k1, p1tbl; rep from ** to last 3 sts, k3.

ROW 3: Sl 1 pwise wyf, p2, *k1tbl, p1, k1tbl, k1; rep from * to 3 sts before m, k1tbl, p1, k1tbl, sl m, knit to m, sl m, k1tbl, p1, k1tbl, **k1, k1tbl, p1, k1tbl; rep from ** to last 3 sts, p3.

ROWS 4–14: Rep Rows 2 and 3 five times, then work Row 2 once more.

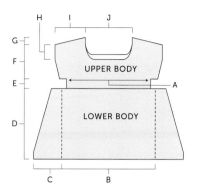

A: 17¾ (19¾, 21¾, 23¾, 25¾)" (45 [50, 55, 60.5, 65.6] cm)

B: 19¾ (21¾, 24, 26¼, 28¼)" (50 [55, 61, 66.5, 72] cm)

C: 6" (15 cm)

D: 14½" (37 cm)

E: 2 (2, 2, 1½, 1½)" (5 [5, 5, 3.8, 3.8] cm)

F: 7 (7½, 8, 8½, 9)" (18 [19, 20.5, 21.5, 23] cm)

G: 1¼" (3.2 cm)

H: 3" (7.5 cm)

I: 6½ (7½, 8¾, 9¾, 10¼)" (16.5 [19, 22, 25, 26] cm)

J: 9¾" (25 cm)

ROW 15: Sl 1 pwise wyf, p2, *k1tbl, p1, k1tbl, k1; rep from * to 3 sts before m, k1tbl, p1, k1tbl, M1R, sl m, knit to m, sl m, M1L, k1tbl, p1, k1tbl, **k1, k1tbl, p1, k1tbl; rep from ** to last 3 sts, p3—2 sts inc'd: 1 st each side panel.

ROW 16: Sl 1 pwise wyb, k2, *p1tbl, k1, p1tbl, p1; rep from * to m, sl m, purl to m, sl m, **p1, p1tbl, k1, p1tbl; rep from ** to last 3 sts, k3.

ROW 17: Sl 1 pwise wyf, p2, *k1tbl, p1, k1tbl, k1; rep from * to m, sl m, knit to m, sl m, **k1, k1tbl, p1, k1tbl; rep from ** to last 3 sts, p3.

ROWS 18–28: Rep Rows 16 and 17 five times, then work Row 16 once more.

ROW 29: Sl 1 pwise wyf, p2, *k1tbl, p1, k1tbl, k1; rep from * to m, M1R, sl m, knit to m, sl m, M1L, **k1, k1tbl, p1, k1tbl; rep from ** to last 3 sts, p3—2 sts inc'd; 1 st each side panel.

ROW 30: Sl 1 pwise wyb, k2, *p1tbl, k1, p1tbl, p1; rep from * to 1 st before m, p1tbl, sl m, purl to m, sl m, p1tbl, **p1, p1tbl, k1, p1tbl; rep from ** to last 3 sts, k3.

ROW 31: Sl 1 pwise wyf, p2, *k1tbl, p1, k1tbl, k1; rep from * to 1 st before m, k1tbl, sl m, knit to m, sl m, k1tbl, **k1, k1tbl, p1, k1tbl; rep from ** to last 3 sts, p3.

ROWS 32–42: Rep Rows 30 and 31 five times, then work Row 30 once more.

Work Rows 1–42 once more, then work Rows 1–14 once more—160 (172, 184, 196, 208) sts: 26 sts each side panel.

NEXT 3 ROWS: Work in patt to m, sl m, knit to m, sl m, work in patt to end.

NEXT ROW: (WS) Work in patt to m, sl m, purl to m, sl m, work in patt to end—lower body measures 14½" (37 cm).

NOTE: *With RS facing, each p1 column in the side panels can be traced back down to a starting yarnover at the base of the column; as you work the following bind-off, drop each single purl stitch and ravel it down to its base.*

NEXT ROW: (RS) BO while dropping sts as foll: *BO in patt until next st on left needle is at top of p1 column (1 st on right needle), drop purl st and ravel it down to its base, use the backward-loop method to CO 1 st onto right needle,

pass 2nd st on right needle over new CO st*, rep from * to * until 1 st rem on left needle before first m, BO center sts kwise (removing first m) to 2nd m; removing 2nd m when you come to it, rep from * to * once more, then BO rem sts.

BACK

UPPER BODY

Work as for upper body of front to end of sleeve incs—139 (151, 165, 179, 191) sts: 15 (15, 16, 17, 17) sts for each sleeve and 109 (121, 133, 145, 157) body sts.

Removing sleeve m on next row as you come to them, work even until piece measures 7 (7½, 8, 8, 8½)" (18 [19, 20.5, 20.5, 21.5] cm) from CO, ending with a WS row.

Shape neck

NEXT ROW: (RS) Work 42 (48, 55, 62, 68) sts in patt and place sts just worked on holder for right shoulder, BO 55 sts, work in patt to end—42 (48, 55, 62, 68) sts rem for left shoulder.

Left shoulder

Work 1 WS row even.

DEC ROW: (RS) K1, ssk, work in patt to end—1 st dec'd. Rep last 2 rows once more—40 (46, 53, 60, 66) sts rem.

Work even until armhole measures 7 (7½, 8, 8½, 9)" (18 [19, 20.5, 21.5, 23] cm) from sleeve CO, ending with a WS row.

Shape shoulder using short-rows as foll:

SHORT-ROW 1: (RS) Knit to last 5 (6, 7, 8, 9) sts, wrap next st, turn.

SHORT-ROW 2 AND ALL WS SHORT-ROWS: Purl to end.

SHORT-ROWS 3, 5, AND 7: Knit to 5 (6, 7, 8, 9) sts before wrapped st, wrap next st, turn.

SHORT-ROW 9: Knit to 10 (11, 12, 14, 15) sts before wrapped st, wrap next st, turn.

NEXT ROW: (WS) Purl to end. BO all sts, working wraps tog with wrapped sts.

Right shoulder

Return 42 (48, 55, 62, 68) right shoulder sts to needle and, with WS facing, rejoin yarn.

Work 1 WS row even.

DEC ROW: (RS) Work in patt to last 3 sts, k2tog, k1—1 st dec'd. Rep last 2 rows once more—40 (46, 53, 60, 66) sts rem.

Work even until armhole measures 7 (7½, 8, 8½, 9)" (18 [19, 20.5, 21.5, 23] cm) from sleeve CO, ending with a RS row. Shape shoulder using short-rows as foll:

SHORT-ROW 1: (WS) Purl to last 5 (6, 7, 8, 9) sts, wrap next st, turn.

SHORT-ROW 2 AND ALL RS SHORT-ROWS: Knit to end.

SHORT-ROWS 3, 5, AND 7: Purl to 5 (6, 7, 8, 9) sts before wrapped st, wrap next st, turn.

SHORT-ROW 9: Purl to 10 (11, 12, 14, 15) sts before wrapped st, wrap next st, turn.

NEXT ROW: (RS) Knit to end. BO all sts, working wraps tog with wrapped sts. Lower body: Work as for front.

FINISHING

Block pieces to measurements, stretching lower edge of each side panel to about 6" (15 cm) wide to open up the drop-stitch detail.

Sew upper body shoulder, underarm, and side seams. Sew tops of side panels tog along their CO edges, keeping tension flexible across tops of drop st columns, and leaving sides of lower body open.

NECKBAND

With 16" needle and RS facing, beg at right shoulder seam, pick up and knit 180 sts evenly spaced around neck edge. Pm and join in the rnd.

Knit 3 rnds.

DEC RND: *K7, k2tog; rep from * to end—160 sts rem.

Knit 3 rnds.

DEC RND: *K6, k2tog; rep from * to end—140 sts rem.

Knit 3 rnds.

DEC RND: *P5, p2tog; rep from * to end—120 sts rem.

Knit 2 rnds.

BO all sts. Weave in ends.

SANTA CRUZ

WRAP

Kephren Pritchett

The Santa Cruz Wrap is a refreshing update on the classic lace stole: it trades frilly lace motifs for a geometric, eye-catching, modern design that uses openwork techniques. This wrap begins with a circular cast-on and is worked in rounds with increases at the corners to create a square.

FINISHED SIZE

18" (45.5 cm) wide and 74" (188 cm) long.

YARN

DK weight (#3)

SHOWN HERE: June Cashmere DK (100% Kyrgyz cashmere; 150 yd [137 m]/ 1¾ oz [50 g]): natural unbleached/ undyed (medium brown), 7 skeins.

NEEDLES

Size U.S. 6 (4 mm): 24" circular (cir) and set of five double-pointed (dpn).

Adjust needle size if necessary to obtain the correct gauge.

NOTIONS

Markers (m); stitch holders.

GAUGE

19 sts and 26 rows = 4" (10 cm) in chart patts.

NOTES

• This shawl begins with a circular cast-on and is worked in rnds with incs at the corners to create a square. When the width of the shawl has been reached, two sides of the square are finished with garter st borders worked perpendicularly to the live sts. The remaining live sts at the top and bottom of the square are worked separately in rows to the ends of the shawl in the chevron pattern with garter st borders.

• Chart A is worked in rnds, and Chart B is worked back and forth in rows.

INSTRUCTIONS

CENTER SQUARE

With dpns and using Emily Ocker's circular method, CO 8 sts—2 sts on each needle.

Place marker (pm) and join in the rnd.

[Work Rnd 1 of Chart A over 2 sts, inc'd to 3 sts] 4 times—12 sts.

Cont in patt through Rnd 72, changing to the cir needle and pm between patt reps when necessary—292 sts: 4 sections of 73 sts each. Break yarn.

Removing m as you go, place first 73 sts on holder—219 sts rem.

SIDE BORDER

Using a provisional method, CO 6 sts onto a dpn.

NEXT ROW: (WS) P1, k5.

NEXT ROW: (RS) K5, ssk (last st on dpn tog with first square st on cir needle)—1 square st joined.

NEXT ROW: (WS) Sl 1 pwise wyf, k5. Rep last 2 rows 72 more times—all sts this side of square have been joined; 146 square sts and 6 border sts rem.

FIRST END

With RS facing, work first 79 sts from Row 1 of Chart B over 6 border sts and 73 center square sts, ending 6 sts before end of chart, place last 73 sts of center square on holder, then use a provisional method to CO 6 sts (which count as last 6 chart sts)—85 sts.

Cont working Chart B until Rows 1–24 have been worked 7 times.

END BORDER

NEXT ROW: (RS) Knit.

EMILY OCKER'S CIRCULAR METHOD

Make a simple loop of yarn with the short end hanging down. With a crochet hook, *draw a loop through main loop, then draw another loop through this loop. Repeat from * for each stitch to be cast on. After several inches have been worked, pull on the short end (shown by arrow) to tighten the loop and close the circle.

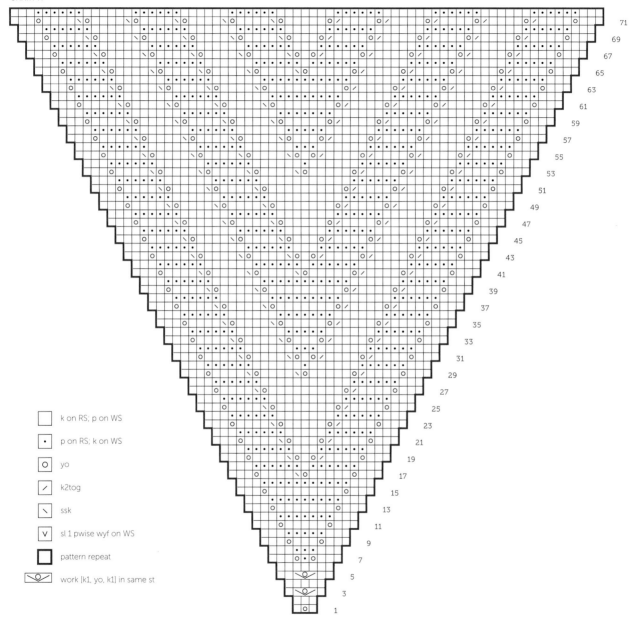

2-st rep inc'd to 73-st rep

k on RS; p on WS

• p on RS; k on WS

O yo

/ k2tog

\ ssk

V sl 1 pwise wyf on WS

pattern repeat

work [k1, yo, k1] in same st

NEXT ROW: (WS) K5, sl 1 pwise wyf, knit to last 6 sts, sl 1 pwise wyf, k5. Rep last 2 rows 4 more times. BO all sts in patt.

SIDE BORDER

Remove waste yarn from provisional CO at end of Chart B's first Row 1 and place 6 CO sts onto dpn. With RS facing, rejoin yarn.

NEXT ROW: (RS) K6.

NEXT ROW: (WS) Sl 1 pwise wyf, k5. Return 73 adjacent held center square sts to cir needle with RS facing.

NEXT ROW: (RS) K5, ssk (last st from dpn tog with first square st on cir needle)—1 square st joined.

NEXT ROW: (WS) Sl 1 pwise wyf, k5.

Rep last 2 rows 72 more times—all sts this side of square have been joined; 6 border sts rem.

SECOND END

Place 6 border sts and 73 rem held center square sts on cir needle, then remove waste yarn from provisional CO and place 6 CO sts onto same needle—85 sts.

Work Rows 1–24 of Chart B 7 times.

END BORDER

NEXT ROW: (RS) Knit.

NEXT ROW: (WS) K5, sl 1 pwise wyf, knit to last 6 sts, sl 1 pwise wyf, k5. Rep last 2 rows 4 more times. BO all sts in patt.

FINISHING

Weave in ends. Block to measurements.

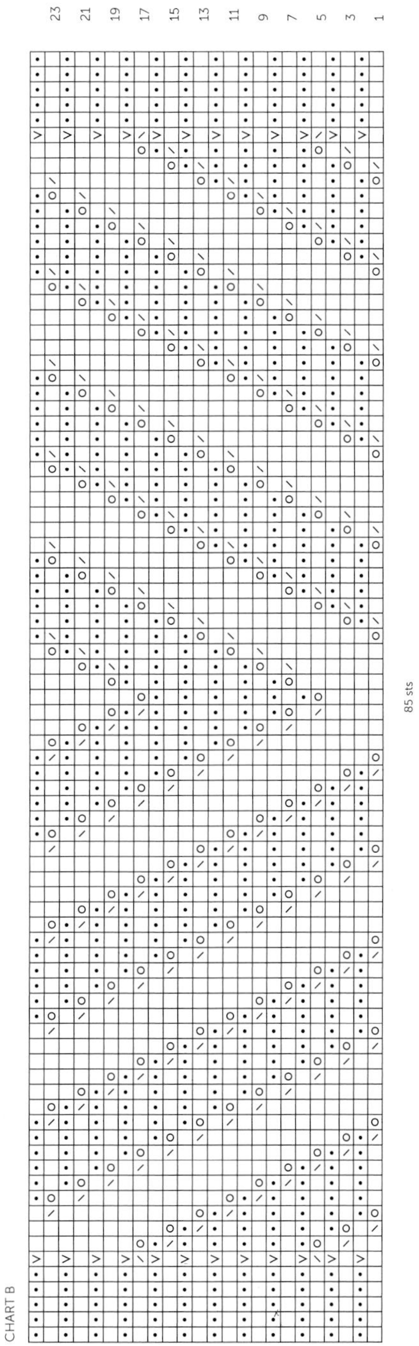

CHART B

85 sts

PEBBLE
BEACH

RUANA

Amy Gunderson

The Pebble Beach Ruana is perfect for all-season layering. This lacy poncho-style garment is made in a breezy, light, 100 percent linen yarn that will keep you cool throughout the spring and summer. Cast on at the back edge, the fabric is worked in one piece up to the shoulders and then divided for the front panels; no sewing is required.

FINISHED SIZE

24½ (27½, 30¾, 33¾)" (61.5 [70, 78, 85.5] cm) wide. Ruana shown measures 24½" (61.5 cm) on a model with a 34" (86.5 cm) bust.

YARN

DK weight (#3)

SHOWN HERE: Fibra Natura Flax (100% linen; 137 yd [125 m]/1¾ oz [50 g]): #18 pewter, 8 (9, 10, 12) skeins. Yarn distributed by Universal Yarn.

NEEDLES

Size U.S. 4 (3.5 mm): 32" circular (cir).

Size U.S. 5 (3.75 mm): 32" cir.

Adjust needle size if necessary to obtain the correct gauge.

NOTIONS

Markers (m); stitch holder; tapestry needle.

GAUGE

21 sts and 21 rows = 4" (10 cm) in Texture st on larger needle.

NOTES

- This ruana is worked in one piece from the lower back edge up and over the shoulders to the lower front edges.

- A cir needle is used to accommodate the large number of sts.

INSTRUCTIONS

STITCH GUIDE

**TEXTURE STITCH
(ODD NUMBER OF STS)**

ROW 1: (RS) Knit.

ROW 2: (WS) *P2tog but do not drop sts from left needle, purl first st again, drop both sts from needle; rep from * to last st, p1.

ROW 3: Knit.

ROW 4: P1, *p2tog but do not drop sts from left needle, purl first st again, drop both sts from needle; rep from * to end.

Rep Rows 1–4 for patt.

BACK

With smaller needle, CO 137 (153, 169, 185) sts. Do not join.

NEXT ROW: (WS) P2, *k1, p1tbl; rep from * to last 3 sts, k1, p2.

NEXT ROW: (RS) Sl 2 pwise wyb, *p1, k1tbl; rep from * to last 3 sts, p1, sl 2 pwise wyb. Rep last 2 rows 2 more times.

NEXT ROW: (WS) P2, [k1, p1tbl] 4 times, place marker (pm), purl to last 10 sts, pm, [p1tbl, k1] 4 times, p2.

NEXT ROW: (RS) Sl 2 pwise wyb, [p1, k1tbl] 4 times, sl m, work Arches for Back chart to m, sl m, [k1tbl, p1] 4 times, sl 2 pwise wyb.

NEXT ROW: (WS) P2, [k1, p1tbl] 4 times, sl m, work chart to m, sl m, [p1tbl, k1] 4 times, p2.

Cont in patt through Row 34 of chart. Change to larger needle.

NEXT ROW: (RS) Work in patt to m, sl m, work Texture st (see Stitch Guide) to m, sl m, work in patt to end. Cont in patt until piece measures 24 (24¾, 25½, 26¼)" (621 [63, 65, 66.5] cm) from CO, ending with a WS row.

NEXT ROW: (RS) Work 63 (71, 79, 87) sts in patt, pm, [k1tbl, M1P] 4 times, k1tbl, M1, k1tbl, [k1tbl, M1P] 4 times, k1tbl, pm, work 63 (71, 79, 87) sts in patt—146 (162, 178, 194) sts.

ARCHES FOR BACK

(Chart with rows numbered on right: 33, 31, 29, 27, 25, 23, 21, 19, 17, 15, 13, 11, 9, 7, 5, 3, 1)

8-st rep

☐	k on RS; pon WS
O	yo
╱	k2togon RS; p2togon WS
╲	ssk
⋏	sl 1 kwise, k2tog, psso
☐	pattern repeat

ARCHES FOR FRONT

8-st rep

- ☐ k on RS; p on WS
- ☐o yo
- ☐⁄ k2tog on RS; p2tog on WS
- ☐\ ssk
- ☐⋏ sl 1 kwise, k2tog, psso
- ☐ pattern repeat

(Chart row numbers shown on right side: 33, 31, 29, 27, 25, 23, 21, 19, 17, 15, 13, 11, 9, 7, 5, 3, 1)

NEXT ROW: (WS) Work in patt to 2nd m, sl m, [p1tbl, k1] 4 times, [p1tbl] 4 times, [k1, p1tbl] 4 times, work in patt to end.

Cont in patt for 2 more rows.

DIVIDE FOR FRONTS

NEXT ROW: (RS) Work in patt to 2nd m, sl m, [k1tbl, p1] 4 times, sl 2 pwise wyb, place next 73 (81, 89, 97) sts on holder for left front—73 (81, 89, 97) sts rem for right front.

RIGHT FRONT

NEXT ROW: (WS) P2, [k1, p1tbl] 4 times, work in patt to end. Cont in patt until piece measures 17 (17¾, 18½, 19¼)" (43 [45, 47, 49] cm) from front divide, ending with a RS row. Change to smaller needle.

NEXT ROW: (WS) Work in patt to m, sl m, purl to m, sl m, work in patt to end.

NEXT ROW: (RS) Work in patt to m, sl m, work Arches for Front chart to m, sl m, work in patt to end.

Cont in patt through Row 34 of chart.

NEXT ROW: (WS) P2, *k1, p1tbl; rep from * to last 3 sts, k1, p2. Next row (RS) Sl 2 pwise wyb, p1, *k1tbl, p1; rep from * to last 2 sts, sl 2 pwise wyb.

Rep last 2 rows 2 more times. BO all sts in patt.

LEFT FRONT

Return 73 (81, 89, 97) held sts to needle and, with RS facing, rejoin yarn.

NEXT ROW: (RS) Sl 2 pwise wyb, [p1, k1tbl] 4 times, sl m, work in patt to end.

Complete as for right front.

FINISHING

Weave in ends. Block to measurements. Beg 9" (23 cm) above lower edge, sew side seams for 4" (10 cm), leaving 11 (11¾, 12½, 13¼)" (28 [30, 31.5, 33.5] cm) unsewn at upper edge for armhole opening.

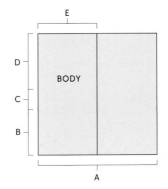

A: 24½ (27½, 30¾, 33¾)" (62 [70, 78, 85.5] cm)

B: 9" (23 cm)

C: 4" (10 cm)

D: 11 (11¾, 12½, 13¼)" (28 [30, 31.5, 33.5] cm)

E: 12¼ (13¾, 15½, 17)" (31 [35, 39.5, 43] cm)

ABBREVIATIONS

beg(s)	begin(s); beginning	**mm**	millimeter(s)	**sl**	slip
BO	bind off	**M1**	make one (increase)	**ssk**	slip, slip, knit
CC	contrast color	**M1L**	make one with left slant (increase)	**st(s)**	stitch(es)
CDD	centered double decrease	**M1P**	make one purlwise (increase)	**St st**	stockinette stitch
cir	circular			**tbl**	through back loop
cm	centimeter(s)	**M1R**	make one with right slant (increase)	**tog**	together
cn	cable needle	**MC**	main color	**w&t**	wrap and turn
CO	cast on	**oz**	ounce	**WS**	wrong side
cont	continue(s); continuing	**p**	purl	**wyb**	with yarn in back
dec(s)('d)	decrease(s); decreasing; decreased	**p1f&b**	purl into the front and back of the same stitch (increase)	**wyf**	with yarn in front
dpn(s)	double-pointed needle(s)			**yd**	yard(s)
foll	follow(s); following	**p2tog**	purl two stitches together (decrease)	**yo**	yarnover
g	gram(s)	**p3tog**	purl three stitches together (decrease)	*****	repeat starting point
inc(s)('d)	increase(s); increasing; increase(d)	**patt(s)**	pattern(s)	*** ***	repeat all instruction between asterisks
k	knit	**pm**	place marker	**( )**	alternate measurements and/or instructions
k1fb	knit into the front and back of the same stitch (increase)	**psso**	pass slipped stitch over	**[ ]**	work instructions within brackets the specified number of times
		pwise	purlwise; as if to purl		
k2tog	knit two stitches together (decrease)	**rem**	remain(s); remaining		
Ktbl	knit the stitch through the back loop.	**rep**	repeat(s); repeating	For terms, abbreviations, and techniques you don't know, please visit our free online knitting glossary at Interweave.com.
kwise	knitwise; as if to knit	**Rev St st**	reverse stockinette stitch	
m	marker	**rnd(s)**	round(s)	
		RS	right side	

YARN RESOURCES

KELBOURNE WOOLENS
www.kelbournewoolens.com

PLYMOUTH YARN COMPANY
www.plymouthyarn.com

TRENDSETTER YARN GROUP
www.trendsetteryarns.com

JUNE CASHMERE
www.junecashmere.com

IMPERIAL YARN
www.imperialyarn.com

BE SWEET
www.besweetproducts.com

MALABRIGO
www.malabrigoyarn.com

JO SHARP
www.knit.net.au

MANOS DEL URUGUAY
www.manosyarns.com

SUGAR BUSH YARNS
www.sugarbushyarns.com

UNIVERSAL YARN
www.universalyarn.com

SKACEL
www.skacelknitting.com

SHIBUI KNITS
www.shibuiknits.com

ANCIENT ARTS YARNS
www.ancientartsfibre.com

WOOLFOLK
www.woolfolkyarn.com

MRS CROSBY
www.mrscrosbyplays.com

BARE NAKED WOOLS
www.barenakedwools.com

VALLEY YARNS
www.yarn.com

ABOUT THE DESIGNERS

GRACE AKHREM is a knitwear designer and native of Los Angeles. She teaches advanced knitting classes nationally, with a focus on technique and design. She is inspired by color, texture, and drape. Grace works as the creative director for the Trendsetter Yarn Group.

VÉRONIK AVERY became a seamstress long before she began to knit. Her experience with sewing clothes and costumes has always influenced her work as a knitwear designer. When she isn't making things out of fiber or fabric, you'll most likely find her in the kitchen, where she eschews sweet things in favor of things savory. Follow her online at www.veronikavery.com.

ANDREA BABB is back home in Canada and exploring the yarn scene in her new hometown of Toronto. You can see what she's working on at www.andreababb.com.

AMANDA BELL lives in New England, where she is outnumbered by her boys. She can be found online at www.applecots.com.

Following a successful management career, **MARY ANNE BENEDETTO** took up her needles full time to pursue a long-standing love of knitwear design. Her aesthetic is rooted in crisp, clean designs that borrow from the classics. When she's not knitting, you can find her skiing, sailing, or trying to keep up with her grown children. Follow along at www.aprioriknits.com.

NORAH GAUGHAN spends almost all of her waking hours knitting or dreaming up new things to knit. She takes a few minutes every day to feed the chickens, collect eggs, and hike with three-year-olds (they are so good at dawdling). New to the craft of spinning, she could easily spin for hours at a time, but she limits herself to twenty minutes per day.

AMY GUNDERSON lives in North Carolina with her husband and their two dogs. She is the creative director for Universal Yarn. When she's not knitting, she is crocheting, weaving, or dreaming of having the time to sew.

SUSANNA IC has an extensive collection of studio arts and art history degrees as well as a rather large yarn stash. Her projects and designs can be found on Ravelry and at www.artqualia.com.

BRISTOL IVY is a knitting designer and teacher from Portland, Maine. Her work focuses on the intersection of classic tailoring and innovative techniques. You can find her at www.bristolivy.com and on Twitter and Instagram as bristolivy.

LANA JOIS loves to knit. Her only regret is that she lives in a land of warm weather that rarely allows her to wear sweaters. Her work has appeared in *Interweave Knits*, *knitscene*, and *Twist Collective*. Look for more of her designs on Ravelry as Lana Jois.

LINDA MARVENG is a Norwegian who loves to design feminine garments, especially with cables or lace. She worked for Rowan Yarns as a design consultant, and she published her first Norwegian knitting book in 2012. She currently designs, proofreads knitting publications, translates patterns, and offers knitting workshops.

KATE GAGNON OSBORN is co-owner of Kelbourne Woolens, distributor of The Fibre Co. yarns, original patterns, and craft accessories. She has coauthored six books and multiple collections of knitting patterns, and her designs have appeared in many magazines. When not working, Kate can be found hanging out with her husband, daughter, and menagerie of pets in their old Victorian home and scheming about which room to renovate next.

KEPHREN PRITCHETT is a knitwear designer and tech editor specializing in seamless construction. She looks for inspiration in the world around her and loves trying out new techniques. You can find more of her work at www.kephrenknittingstudio.com.

Originally from the Midwest, **AMANDA SCHEUZGER** now lives in beautiful Maine, where she spends her free time knitting socks in preparation for the cold New England winter. Find Amanda online at www.handmaineknits.com and on Instagram as handmaineknits.

SARAH SOLOMON lives in New York City, where she designs and teaches knitting. She blogs about knitting at www.intothewool.wordpress.com. You can find her patterns on Ravelry as Sarah Solomon Designs.

EMMA WELFORD is a knitwear designer from western Massachusetts. By day, she works in social media; by night, she knits, spins, and plays post-apocalyptic video games. You can find her online at www.emmawelford.com.

ENHANCE YOUR WARDROBE
WITH MORE SOPHISTICATED STITCHES

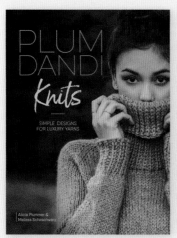

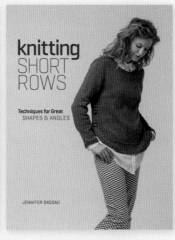